EDITORIAL

FIONA SAMPSON

The winter solstice is always a good time to reflect on seasonality, and the inevitability of change. Who can miss it, as we dive deeper into the cold – but the days get longer? Luckily, we've some fine poets to help with these reflections. C.K. Williams's richly nuanced account of the anxieties he associates with getting older was a great success as the Poetry Society's Annual Lecture, making us laugh and cry – and think. For age may be a cultural but it is also a biological fact. So this issue also includes a triptych observing seasonal change in the natural world. Fleur Adcock and Richard Kerridge write about metamorphoses in the animal kingdom, while Ruth Padel offers a sneak preview of her forthcoming book about migration at every level, from the cellular to the societal.

Then seasons, too, can be cultural as much as biological. Mevlut Ceylan, of the new Turkish Cultural Centre in London, gives us a taster of the work of Turkish poets living and working outside that country, in the cultural melting pot of the Balkans. These surprisingly large communities are, of course, evidence of history's changeability. Yet, though they may be more violent, historical eras are no more arbitrary than cultural fashions. Also in Centrefold, Evan Jones introduces the first of our 'Reputations Recouped', which not surprisingly belongs to a woman: the Canadian modernist Anne Wilkinson. Her death at fifty-one came just at the start of the cultural revolution that was the Sixties. We might also suggest that early death disproportionately affects the reputation of women poets: often later starters than their male peers, they may need an older age free of domestic responsibilities to develop an equivalent body of work.

Reputations are made and broken by these concatenations of accidental circumstances. No such accident bars us from enjoying a stunning set of poems: from Anne Carson, deepening the elegiac work of her recent and extraordinary *Nox*, to Stanley Moss's philosophical meditations, by way of signature pieces by Patience Agbabi, Selima Hill and Kathleen Jamie, among many others. And we keep abreast of the great, and long-awaited, news of Tomas Tranströmer's Nobel laureateship with Alan Brownjohn's review of Robin Fulton and Bloodaxe's prescient reissue of the complete works. Eventually, it seems, *rota fortuna* does throw up the right result. And here is one all poetry lovers can celebrate.

CONTRIBUTORS

Fleur Adcock's most recent collection is *Dragon Talk* (Bloodaxe, 2010). **Patience Agbabi** was awarded a Grant for the Arts (2010) to write a contemporary interpretation of *The Canterbury Tales*. **Marianne Boruch**'s *The Book of Hours* was recently published (Copper Canyon). She teaches at Purdue University but is currently a Fulbright Scholar at Edinburgh University. **Niall Campbell** received an Eric Gregory Award in 2011. **Anne Carson**'s *Nox* appeared from *New Directions* in 2010. She won the T.S. Eliot Prize in 2000. **Anthony Costello** is a poet and gardener. **Douglas Houston**'s Selected Poems appeared from Shoestring this year. **Kathleen Jamie**'s new collection will be published in 2012. She teaches at Stirling University. **Martin Harrison**'s latest volume is *Wild Bees: New and Selected Poems* (University of Western Australia Press and Shearsman). **John Haynes**'s *You* was shortlisted for the T.S. Eliot Prize. *Letter to Patience* won the Costa Poetry Award. **Selima Hill**'s poems are from her forthcoming collection *People Who Like Meatballs* (Bloodaxe). **Tim Liardet**'s latest collection is *The Storm House* (Carcanet 2011). **A.A. Marcoff** is a regular contributor to the haiku magazines, and has lived in Africa, Iran, France and Japan. **Toby Martinez De Las Rivas** has received an Eric Gregory award (2005) and an Andrew Waterhouse award (New Writing North, 2008) and had a pamphlet published by Faber (2009). **Gonzalo Melchor**'s translations also appear in *Poetry London* and *Poetry* (US). **Christopher Middleton** lives and works in the US but is arguably the last remaining British modernist. **Stanley Moss** recently published *God Breaketh Not All Men's Hearts Alike: New and Later Collected Poems* (Seven Stories Press); his most recent UK volume is *Rejoicing: New and Collected Poems* (Anvil). **Estill Pollock**'s books include *Relic Environments Trilogy* (Cinnamon Press 2011). **Neil Powell**'s seventh collection, *Proof of Identity*, is published by Carcanet in February. **Sam Riviere** co-edits *Stop Sharpening Your Knives*, and received a 2009 Eric Gregory Award. Faber published his pamphlet in 2010. **Luis Rosales** (1910-1992), one of the most important poetic voices of the Spanish Generation of 1936, was awarded the Cervantes Prize. **Anne Rouse**'s latest book is *The Upshot: New and Selected Poems* (Bloodaxe, 2008). **Maurice Rutherford**'s New and Selected, *And Saturday is Christmas*, was published in March 2011 by Shoestring. **David Tait** co-founded the Leeds Independent Presses Poetry Festival; his pamphlet is reviewed on p.102. **Tony Williams**'s *All the Rooms of Uncle's Head* (Nine Arches, 2011) is a PBS Pamphlet Choice.

Contents

Volume 101:4 Winter 2011

Editorial

Poems

6	Anne Carson	Powerless Structures Fig. 11 (SANNE)
8	Kathleen Jamie	The Galilean Moons
10	Douglas Houston	The Balcony, Back Of Van Beuningenstraat
11	Stanley Moss	Anatomy Lessons
		Listening To Water
13	Carol Rumens	The Pharaoh's Pyramid Text
		from Dante's Purgatorio
18	Maurice Rutherford	Kinderwelt
19	Marianne Boruch	First
20	Toby Martinez de las Rivas	Penitential Psalm
21	Anne Rouse	High Wall
22	Selima Hill	I Couldn't Stand The Smell Of The Pinks
		My Adoration
		Modest Acts Of Extreme Slowness
25	John Haynes	That Double Bass
26	Martin Harrison	White Flowers
		April
29	Neil Powell	Hotel Codan, 1962
30	Niall Campbell	Kirilov
31	Tony Williams	A Bouquet For Pauline Viardot
34	Luis Rosales	What Is Not Remembered
35	Tim Liardet	Grunt
36	David Morley	Hassle
37	Patience Agbabi	Unfinished Business
38	Anthony Costello	Mutual Attraction
39	Christopher Middleton	The Gnats
40	A A Marcoff	land, & the river
41	Estill Pollock	At The Window, Last Night's Words, Ashen
42	David Tait	On Being Trapped Inside A Puddle
43	Sam Riviere	My Face Saw Her Magazine

Centrefold

The Poetry Society Annual Lecture

46   C.K. Williams   *On Being Old*

The Seasonal World

60   Richard Kerridge   *The Season Of The Newts*
62   Ruth Padel   from *The Mara Crossing*
70   Fleur Adcock   from *Kiss The Winged Joy As It Flies*
    73   Mevlut Ceylan   Turkish Poets Of The Balkans

Reputations Recouped

80   Evans Jones   Anne Wilkinson

Reviews

86   Alan Brownjohn reviews Tranströmer, Gorbanevskaya and Schnackenberg
89   Chloe Stopa-Hunt reviews Burnside and Greenlaw
93   Steven Matthews reviews Oswald
95   Carol Rumens reviews Bennet, Collins and Warner
98   Lachlan Mackinnon reviews Wicks, Duran, Chase, Dugdale, Grovier and Tait
103   Tracy Ryan reviews Campbell, Lleshanaku and Riley
106   W.N. Herbert reviews Lynch and Williams
110   Todd Swift reviews Pato, Caley, Bose, Bentley, Holloway-Smith and Wright
114   David Morley reviews Nagra, Higgins and Breeze
118   Leah Fritz reviews Pindar, Potts, Evans, Eaves and Williams
122   Sarah Wardle reviews Flynn, Black, Quinn, Darcy and Montague

Endpapers

126   Ruth O'Callaghan   *The Big Stage*

POEMS

the hinge, little cry that won't uncry itself –

– *Marianne Boruch*

Anne Carson
Powerless Structures Fig. 11 (SANNE)

HER FUNERAL
is in Sankt Johannes nine years after his.

THAT GOLDSMUGGLER
she fell in love with in Amsterdam is how he appears in her eulogy.

BLUSH NO
I never saw her blush.

OPEN BOAT
driving rain we go on a tour of the harbour she sits unprotected smoking.

I FIRST
met her on the telephone you don't know me she said but your brother has
just died in my bathroom.

APPARENTLY THEY'D
been married 17 years.

WHAT'S THAT
sound the dog oh you have a dog yes we have a dog no *I* have a dog.

HER STORIES
of his stubborness fears Xmas dinners dope dog kindness to her mad mother
and refusal to talk about the past his beard that he would shave off when he
got some money he never did.

ENGLISH IDIOMS
she usually avoids he was the light of my life is one she does use.

SHE CALLS
in tears tears fill up the phone.

THAT ONE
she said she was a bartender in Amsterdam and he walked in that one I want
to marry.

I CLEANED
him I keep hearing when he died her clipped phrases who else between drags
should do it.

TEARS FILL
up the phone I empty it.

WE WALK
by the canal swans drift down the water one leg trailing one leg tucked up
behind.

SHE GOT
in the ambulance went to the hospital and there insisted on washing the body
who else should do it she said.

THE GERUNDIVE
is a verb form expressing obligation or necessity three little steps up no steps
down.

SHE DIES
in April 2010 of alcohol and indescribable longing.

MOST PEOPLE
blush before death.

SHE JUST
steps off.

Kathleen Jamie
The Galilean Moons

for Nat Jansz

Low in the south sky shines
the stern white lamp
of planet Jupiter. A man
on the radio said
it's uncommonly close,
and sequestered in the telescope lens
it's like a compère, spotlit,
driving its borrowed light
out to all sides equally
while, set in a row in the dark
beyond its blaze,
like seed-pearls,
or coy new talents
awaiting their call onstage
– what must be, surely,
the Galilean moons.

In another room,
my children lie asleep, turning
as Earth turns, growing
into their own lives, leaving me
a short time to watch, eye
to the eye-piece,
how a truth unfolds –
how the moonlets glide
out of their chance alignment,
each again to describe
around its shared host its own
unalterable course. Tell me,

Galileo, is this
what we're working for?
– the knowledge that in just
one Jovian year
the children will be gone
uncommonly far, their bodies
aglow, grown, talented – become
mere bright voice-motes
calling from the opposite
side of the world...
what else would we want
our long-sighted instruments
to assure us of ? I'd like
to watch for hours, see
what you old astronomers
apprehended for the first time,
bowed to the inevitable...

but it's late already:
the next day's obligations
pluck at my elbow
like an infant who needs his mother,
next-door's dog barks,
and cloud arrives, distilled,
it appears, out of nothing.

Douglas Houston
The Balcony, Back Of Van Beuningenstraat

for Paul Evans

On clear summer nights it frames
Cassiopeia and the Plough
with the North Star centre stage,
a darkness for entering
in peace and the hope of peace
at daylight, to meet morning
opening endlessly over
this triangle of gardens
where the courtship of magpies
comes and goes in the flashes
of heraldic black and white
in green depths just beyond reach
from the balcony's frontier
with gravity.
          Its steel rail
bears cantilevered troughs
where hanging gardens flourish,
the lavender and parsley,
coriander, sage, and mint,
untended and rife, spilling
swags of tiny leaves on air
three floors above thriving lawns
and bushes, dense undergrowth,
each leaf and blade tumescent,
glutted with sunlight and rain,
private rainforest domain
of the emerald-yellow bird
that comes to perch on the rail.

Stanley Moss
Anatomy Lessons

I
At Piazza Santa Croce
I bought a print for less than the cost of a gelato,
an etching made when vivisection was a sin:
a battle in a vineyard: long-haired naked men
against long-haired naked men, Tuscans
cut open, dissected with sabres, crossbows and axes.
They do not fight half lusting for each other.
They do not take pleasure in their nakedness as bathers do
or fight for a cause, city or God,
or over a lover removed from the scene.
There is the artist's cause—to show flesh unresurrected,
how men look, stripped to bones and innards.

II
With their book on love, *The Neck-Ring of the Dove*,
Muslims came to Florence from Córdoba,
dressed lords and ladies in gold and silver
brocades and taffetas—their poet-physicians taught
how naked bodies looked in life and death,
kissed and torn to pieces on earth, in hell and paradise.

III
These days they pass a camera with ease
down the throat and out the anus, taking silent movies
of what was thought divine. Note: the sacred heart,
masked surgeons watch vital signs, seldom genuflect.
There is the poetry of sonar imaging, the heart, the kidneys,
the diseased prostate doomed to shipwreck
in the blood and urine of mothering seas.
X-rated and X-rayed, the body is sacred, love is still an art
some call "praying": lying down, standing up, or on their knees,
whatever the place, the time of day or night they please,
when the body lets the soul do whatever it please.

Listening To Water

Water wanted to live.
It went to the sun,
came back laughing.
Water wanted to live.
It went to a tree
struck by lightning.
It came back laughing.
It went to blood. It went to womb.
It washed the face of every living thing.
A touch of it came to death, a mould.
A touch of it was sexual, brought life to death.
It was Jubal, inventor of music,
the flute and the lyre.

"Listen to waters," my teacher said,
"then play the slow movement
of Schubert's late *Sonata in A*,
it must sound like the first bird
that sang in the world."

Carol Rumens
The Pharaoh's Pyramid Text

When the king wants the war,
the soldier wants the war.
When the soldier wants the war as the king wants it,
the war loves the soldier.
It loves the kingly soldier, and the king's god loves him.
The army shines from the south, its swelling river
promises mercy to the hard fields.
The soldier shines from the south, he wants the kingdom
as the swelling river wants it when it climbs
over the rocks and washes the hard fields
with dawn, and scatters grain-stars: when the soldier
wants to become the seed, the soldier sows the kingdom
in corn so tall it reaches the king's shoulder
and bends its ears as he whispers
Bring me the bread of war. Bring me the soldier.

Canto 27
from Dante's Purgatorio

For Maurice Rutherford

It was first light where light's first Creator
had spilled His blood: time's level scale-pans soared
above the Ebro; noon at the equator

saw Ganges simmering: thus the fallen world.
Here, the sun was leaving us. Beyond
the barrier flames, God's happy angel carolled.

The hymn he sang, 'Corde beati mundo',
made purer by the crystal of his voice,
left our own small voices thick with wonder.

As we came closer, his was grave advice.
'Holy Souls, you must pass through this fire.
Keep listening as you painfully advance:

You'll hear the music that you most desire.'
My hands stretched up, white-knuckling each other.
Bodies like mine were twisting on that pyre.

My good guides turned to me. Virgil, my father,
murmured, 'Punishment, dear child, is not
death. If you're to die, why did I bother

to help you conquer Geryon? Think of that
rough ride! I swear these flames could interweave
your hair a thousand years, and you'd meet God unhurt.

Come. Test them with a corner of your sleeve.'
I was ashamed, but didn't dare to touch;
stricken with guilt, but didn't dare to move.

My lack of fortitude perturbed my teacher.
'That wall,' he said, 'Is all that stands between
yourself and Heaven's light – your Beatrice.'

Once, when the fabled mulberry lost her green,
the dying Pyramus raised his head on hearing
Thisbe's name, and found her face. So when

those sounds were uttered, sweet, familiar, searing,
I looked up, knowing all my obstinacy
undone. My master nodded. 'So we're staying?'

He smiled. As if I'd been a child of three,
mollified by an apple. We moved forward –
Virgil first – and Statius, following distantly.

Once in the flames, I gasped, I would have arrowed
into the nearest pool of boiling glass
to cool my skin. My gentle father borrowed

consoling fictions: 'Beatrice's eyes
already shine on us!' We heard again
the angel's guiding voice: it rose and rose,

and we emerged where our ascent began.
'Venite, benedicte Patris mei'
welled from a radiance that outshone the sun.

I had to shade my eyes and look away.
'Hurry, before the west is plunged in darkness!'
I turned, my body blocking the last ray,

to mount that steep stair cut through the crevasse.
A short way up, my shadow disappeared,
And night, we knew, had overtaken us.

Each swiftly chose a step, and made his bed.
Our strength was sapped, if not our willingness.
We were like mountain-goats who'd leaped and veered

from ledge to ledge but now, in sheltered grass,
watched by the shepherd leaning on his crook,
would feed and browse. I thought how herdsmen pass

their nights al fresco, caring for their flock.
My shepherds lay nearby. Immense bright stars
filled the small sky between the parted rock.

I contemplated them until my gaze
dissolved in sleep – sleep with its curious skill
for revelations which foretell the day's.

The same time as Cytherea's brimming shell
flooded the mountain from the east, I dreamed
about a woman, young and beautiful,

who sang: 'Whoever asks my name, I'm named
Leah. My hands are busy weaving flowers
for necklaces – and yet my sister's charmed

by simple looking. Rachel sits for hours
content with her reflection. So we share
the fruits of action's, and of vision's, powers.'

Day-break, with that magnificence of cheer
well-known to travellers home, whose spirits lift
higher each day to feel their goal so near,

coloured the sky. Night's shadows went adrift
with my departing dreams, and I awakened
to see my masters had already left.

'That apple, for which many boughs are broken
by ravenous mortals, will today ensure
that you are sweetly feasted.' I was shaken

by Virgil's promise. With each step, the more
desire sprang up in me. I seemed to grow
wings; I'd soon be light enough to soar!

The stairs had rushed away, and hung below,
when Virgil fixed me with his eye, and said
'My child, I understand I cannot go

beyond this point. How far you've travelled, tried
by flames that pass, and flame unending! Skill
and insight fitted me to be your guide:

but now let pleasure take on Virgil's role.
See the great sun that lights your forehead, see
grasses and trees and flowers in the rich soil

of infinite blooming. You're at liberty,
after your long, hard climb, to be delighted,
until the lovely eyes, which summoned me,

and by whose tearfulness I was conscripted
into your service, come to you again,
shining with happiness restored, completed.

From me, expect no further word or sign.
Stand tall and free: your will is now your own.
Trust it, as I trust you. I now assign
to your self-governance, the mitre and the crown.'

Maurice Rutherford
Kinderwelt

When Gerda Bluhm was getting on for nine
and Myra not yet two, a bond was sealed
as sometimes happens in a family where
the elder daughter finds herself in line
to play the rôle of mother and to yield
to vulnerable siblings all the care
an absent parent might. So, Gerda led,
and Myra absorbed all her idol taught
by sheer example, higher intellect,
a love that grew. They neither of them wed.
They're in their eighties now and time has caught
at Gerda's hem. Sometimes, she can't connect.
The care-nurse comes, a youngster full of praise
for Gerda's answers to her "little quiz",
"That's good! Now spell 'world' backwards." Myra says,
but softly, "Backwards, *stimmt*, that's how it is."

Marianne Boruch
First

it's given. Then made.
Until the dying one says *Dream, undream me.*

Fragment to pattern, to inscription
in dust, on leaf, across any
cardboard box in the dumpster.

He climbs a ladder to scrape then paint
one side of the house each summer into fall.
Or he skips a few years. Another winter
ringed by a keyhole. And the door, what of

the hinge, little cry that won't uncry itself —

Toby Martinez de las Rivas
Penitential Psalm

Out of the shallows, horizonless, unbroken, the impenitent, vertical body

tenders its asperities

     to blinding waters.

                    Tenderly

None to anoint it, looking out towards Huish and the dismal stratocumuli.

O, hark at! The helicopterish *whap | whap* of goose wings.

         Shall I thrust

my own head under, inhale the shattered meniscus,

the third clause held indefinitely to spite your transformational grammar?

                ghost-cases of larvae fixed to stems
                in the vacancy of self-possession

Fierce joy that is like retching, undo me. As a dead polity,

brick by brick, stitch by stitch, the squat, feudal tower at Langport,

or the drowned mole in this baptismal water, claws subtly demonstrative

of admonishment, supplication, *woefully arrayed.*

                My tender heartroot for thee brake:

My tender heartroot for you in the brake of thorns,

  and the desperate purchase of this falling metre, Laura.

Anne Rouse
High Wall

Behind a bricked-in yard you could hear the alley
where lorries backed in, to the kvetching of a drill.
Damp ivy grew over the wall, and I set out marigolds,
little suns against the grime, and forgot to replace them when they died.

Nothing ever went wrong — the sounds grew thin, enfolded;
the windows stuck shut, the bricks stood worn, and high —
but in time I climbed out, into nothing's weeds and blight,
and felt what was hidden: a tearing anger at the living, and found

a gash in the earth, a fallow groove, and turned up the ground,
to bring on the dry, flecked seeds of grass,
the blazoning tint of which could be seen, newly insistent,
in the loam this morning: an undulant, unyielding green,
when I crouched down and looked, with you, and the child.

Selima Hill
I Couldn't Stand The Smell Of The Pinks

I couldn't stand the smell of the pinks
and I honestly used to think I was going crazy

and I probably *did* go crazy in a way
because during the day I was terrified of the night

and during the night I was terrified of the day
and then in the *day* I was terrified of the *day*

so probably, yes, I did go a little crazy
and that was when the elephant appeared,

colossal and refulgent, at my side
(colossal but without any fuss)

and soon we started walking down the road,
nice and slow, like people carrying buckets.

My Adoration

Something like a sofa made of buns
is settling itself backwards on my lap –
or trying to: it doesn't understand
it's not a baby, it's an elephant,
not to mention warble-flies, so, no,
it's never going to work, I'm afraid,
much as I would like to say it will,
much as I would like – would love! – to cuddle him,

to gaze into his little seed-like eyes
and kiss his scratchy cheek, but it won't work;
being sort of sat on by a sofa –
a large unhappy sofa with a tail,
that dreams of growing up to be a ship
whose wake of gold will grasp the sea and hurtle it
out across the sky until it shatters
and showers us with jewels – doesn't work,

is never going to work, but the elephant,
refusing to accept that his behind
is not a perfect fit, the sobbing elephant
seems to think *I've ruined his life* –
which only goes to show how wrong I was
to think, to even dream, that an elephant
could possibly begin to understand
the quality of my adoration.

Modest Acts Of Extreme Slowness

I thought you were nice,
I thought it was all my fault;
I thought it was all my fault right from the beginning
and nothing really mattered except you,
I thought you were Mr Right
but I was wrong;
I thought you could play the piano but I was wrong,
I thought that being attractive wasn't important
as long as you played the piano but I was wrong;

I thought I could somehow entrust you with my body
like golden soup entrusted to warmed bowls,
that if I grabbed your head and whacked or slapped it
it'ld change your ways; that men will always thank me;
that married couples in their beds perform
modest acts of extreme slowness;
that making love with you would be the same
as making love with lots of little kittens;
I thought I heard them purring. I was wrong.

John Haynes
That Double Bass

You never had much time
for Charlie Kunz,
those long pedal-held-down

bi-boom and plink-up rhythms
he didn't make
himself but had thrum-

down-deep faked
by some studio
double bass,

"that people don't even know
is even *there*, John!"
you'd say creasing your face – old pro

to the ends
of your fingertips, and beyond.

Martin Harrison
White Flowers

The air the wind the outside and outsize
of what's possible and imaginable
clear and clean endeavour into the atmosphere
of light on dark and glittering spaces
where crimson rosellas swerve sideways
into cascades of down-hanging white flowers
they land whistling in that snowy down
that galactic spray of weeping branches
now revealing themselves in an entirety
of whitenesses for a few days in a
suddenness which takes my breath away
because the enormity of the thousands
of pale-yellow-hearted four-petaled flowerlets
is an act of exposure on so huge a scale –
and to what? the wind, the next moon,
the rain-streaked winter light? the sun? –
and because the suddenness is
what suddenly and surreptitiously
strikes you (invisible, unthought
awareness) as the same naked revealedness
of your lover beneath you, beside
you or above you caught there
where humanness itself is flowering light
ecstatic with joy in the act of love

April

The sunset's pink patches

trails happening through clouds

a slow dissolve

the last ray tilted

bursting out against the black

ridge with its silhouetted

stick-trees

picked out upon momentary

lemon – two or three seconds

of it –

where instantly a metal wall

stands out whitely

revealing the old shed

in a kind of hole between trees

never before noticed

a split second

re-organising

the world

anchoring it in

a single thought

The fire's wood smoke

drift through the branches

heat against the cold

that sudden sense of reversal

suddenly, more heat focussed

in a circle

yellow flames swarming

like a hand's palpitations

touching flesh massaging it

dangerous

beyond words

the slope is a whole incline

but the fire-bomb's

more intense at its heart

than any colour

beyond colour

how the heat takes over

as if the centre

must now fight against the

grains of darkness

which hang over cold, dry earth

no, a singular thought

of fade-out

in which energy slips

through the nerves' network

because it's like the end

unspeakable sadness

because it's the end

for weeks you were dying

(I can't bear it, even

to say it

glowing with them and

and against them

covering the intensity

in a war with the rainbow

spectred

across the ridge

focussed on flames upshooting

from branches leaves twigs dust

holding heat together

converting them

in that skein

of fire

into immeasurables

and unknowns

Neil Powell
Hotel Codan, 1962

With its perkily assertive fifties lowercase 'd',
The hotel's sign has just gone out of date.
Otherwise, it's as the man from Tuborg said:
All glassy restraint, and the best view in town.

I must earn the freedom of this Nordic city,
Its green oxidised roofs and gulping gargoyles.
The English bookshop has next month's Penguins,
But I'm learning new words: *smørrebrød*, *pilsner*, *duvet*.

On a pleasure-boat cruising the blue canals,
An olive-skinned boy my age is collecting fares:
Youthful outsiders, we exchange complicit smiles.
Lights dance in the water by the floating tattooist.

Dinner tonight in the rooftop restaurant
Where an elderly pianist, Viennese and dapper,
Plays lollipops spiked with melancholia.
Old Europe's sadness drifts on the darkened sea.

Niall Campbell
Kirilov

The wolf stalked the winter forest,
its ribs a veiled fist. Tasted nothing
but the long empty plate of snow –
listening to the willow-weed,
the birch, the wind that runs through them.
Deciding just the same, that wolf
should be the last taste on a wolf's lips.

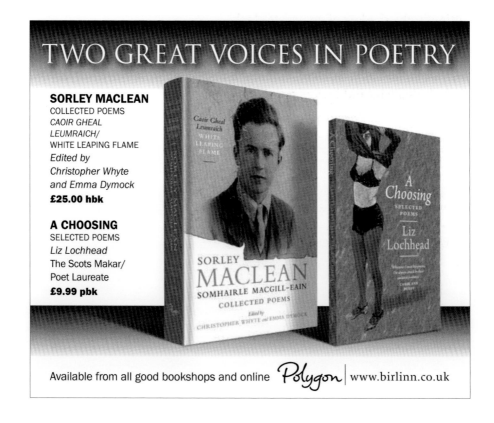

Tony Williams
A Bouquet For Pauline Viardot

It is not 1843, the premiere of *Lucia*, bursting forth
in Petersburg, the dawning of her lucid Russian day,
Chopin still alive, composing preludes
in honour of the smell of the earth
and the sight of bare trees against the opal sky
in the carriage, very early in the morning;
the numberless, unnecessary, splendid parades,
the Second Empire still to come; and Eugene,
breathless, drunk, the belt of his greatcoat hanging down,
dancing along the bank of the Neva to her song.

It's 1859, she's back in Paris singing *Euridice* by Glück,
who's dead, as Chopin is dead and gone:
she thinks of him, remembers a drawing of a human brain,
sitting in the shadow of an ornate clock,
in a dark room full of costly clutter,
with high ceilings, waiting to go on,
waiting for the men to come their flowers,
their doffed hats and invitations to dine.

She manages a little scale under her breath,
the glass clouds, and Eugene in Russia
thinks of her – perhaps it was a phrase from that little consumptive waif,
that canary, the songbird in her yellow dress –
above the clatter of the tables – and turns on his heel.
Michael – did I ever tell you – what about a little game of faro –
first, let's eat! They'll set us out a table – Viardot –
the singer – a whole month I was in love,
on the strength of one performance which she gave!

The lamplight smears and shines across crystal
in a voice-filled hall and the frown of a man tuning his cello,
while she in the gloom swallows the silence with a smile,
moving her hand towards an impossible chord.

Late elevations of tone, a key-change,
an impresario, spreading his hands wide,
something in his face physically strange,
and the sound of a scuffle in the street outside:
hare with gooseberry sauce – pig's feet –
a rattled old woman clearing her throat –
another three bottles of champagne –
the Empire's stars and the sharp horizon
and the cigar's smoke troubling my heart
that morning. A woodcutter drove by on an empty cart
as I sat on the wall of the wharf –
but I'm repeating myself. Turning up in a phalanx of swells and whores
(those rooms where high society reaches round to its tail)
– raised glasses, voices, downcast eyes – whirls and spills –
hands of cards, quarrels, assignations – all
of it in movement, all of it unclear.

And her, Viardot who will outlive Victoria,
a waxen image of calm in the tremulous room,
dispensing a glance on the footmen, the silverware,
thinking of the first line in a song and the difficult rhyme.
Fortunes capsizing: the dreadful, sleepless faces, the picking up of chairs,
the chimes of yesterday – exits, the big stampede.
Settling a debt with a retired officer of guards
while his comrade strokes a tart's hair
who lies softly weeping, and that fat little author
murdering the language with his tongue
– that's the accompaniment to her song.

No one hears it but me. The closed door, the ebony panels, the gilt
and the tall, sad windows and the brindle cat –
the fire resplendent in its vast proscenium
blushing its last bow to the empty room –
her pearly hands moving listlessly over the lacquer
and the brilliant, remorseless keys – she sings to herself
softly and no one hears it, not I, Eugene, so far away across
all the indignant, superannuated bishoprics, sending her roses
like all the other roses – and another – and another –
chess and peppermint tea, the smell of leather,
a horse's nose distorted in a lustrous tuba –
swamps and stern forestations, water rails,
partridge, snipe, woodcock and grouse,
juvenile storks and God knows what else,
tortoiseshell, alabaster, tuberculosis...

Enfin, a snowdrift of last thoughts, those ornate, flower-angled brooches,
though we are very far from the end – boas
and scientific breakthroughs, Frenchmen
writing indecent books, attempting the Matterhorn –
private theatres, manic depressive maids,
pet names for minerals, rhodomontade
as a way of being – rum and soda water, syrup of quince –
these to Madame Viardot with my compliments.

Luis Rosales
What Is Not Remembered

To be joyful again we
only needed the good luck
of remembering.
                We searched
inside our hearts for our memories.
Maybe happiness has no history.
As we gazed within
we were both silent.
                    Your eyes were
like a still herd
that brings its shiver under the shade
of a poplar tree.
                Silence
was stronger than our effort.
                        The sky
darkened for ever.
We could not remember it again.
In the sea the breeze was a blind child.

Translated by Gonzalo Melchor

Tim Liardet
Grunt

Your foot's shy of the rowing machine's baggy loop left by Babe Ruth;
his feet twice the length, three times the width,
that big toe, the left one, an embarrassment.
He was Six-two, weighed two hundred and fifteen pounds;
his arms would have reached around you twice.
What he has in body, though, you make up for in subtlety,
in charisma, in wit and in charm, you think,
even though a hundred pounds lighter, even though Five-six;
when you row you grunt, as if to inhabit the bigger grunt;
as if the bigger grunt might propel you like a sail.

It goes on, the war between big and littler men.
Okay, you say. The ghost goes through its work-out.
For its every long pull on the oar – from air-grip to waist –
you have to pull five or more to keep up with the pace.

David Morley
Hassle

The mush savo kek se les the juckni-wast oprey
his jib and his zi is keck kosko to jal adrey sweti.

The man who has not the whip-hand of his tongue
and temper is not fit to go into company but Mike
is Mike is Mike, and all's thrown from horizon to sky
when his whip-hand's wired by White Lightning and Rye.
That is how we imagine him. Unfit for human society.
Mike thinks the planet's one long bloody hassle.
Constellations spinning in the wing-mirror of his van
whether police cars or pole stars Mike's heading home

to the full beam of a haulage depot, the sump and spill
of his caravan site, to the tilted mirror of a bottle,
the windscreen smash of hangover, to the oil chamber
of solicitors' chambers, the handbrake turn of high court,
wheel spins of reporters. The exhaust of exhaustion
after hours haggling and hustling over access to his children.

Patience Agbabi
Unfinished Business

> *Conveniently, cowardice and forgiveness look identical at a certain distance. Time steals your nerve. – Jonathan Nolan,* Memento

That night, it rained so hard
it was biblical. The Thames sunk the promenade,
spewing up so much low life.
It's a week since they beat up my wife,
put five holes in my daughter. I know who they are.
I know why. I'm three shots away from the parked car
in a blacked-out car park. My wife cries,
Revenge too sweet attracts flies.
Even blushed with bruises she looks good. She's lying
on the bed, next to me. *Honey, I'm fine.*
Tonight I caught her, hands clasped, kneeling,
still from a crime scene.
I didn't bring my wife to Gravesend for this.
What stops me, cowardice?
None of them, even Joe, has the right to live.
How can I forgive?

How can I forgive
none of them? Even Joe has the right to live.
What stops me, cowardice?
I didn't bring my wife to Gravesend for this
still from a crime scene.
Tonight I caught her, hands clasped, kneeling
on the bed next to me. *Honey, I'm fine.*
Even blushed with bruises she looks good. She's lying.
Revenge too sweet attracts flies
in a blacked-out car park. My wife cries.
I know why. I'm three shots away from the parked car
put five holes in my daughter. I know who they are.
It's a week since they beat up my wife,
spewing up so much low life
it was biblical. The Thames sunk the promenade
that night, it rained so hard.

Anthony Costello
Mutual Attraction

It seems a long time ago
that we climbed to the spiralling top
of Switzerland's Geneva campanile,
the name of the Church I forget
(do you remember?); I remember
the intervale between the rocketing
Jet d'eau in the quiet Lake's water,
the wind-gap of the concrete vault
below our feet; I never told you
(and it has been lost since)
that I wrote a poem about you
that could only be expressed
in magnificent death-resulting leaps
(how romantic!); there were no steps
from towers, just a slow moving
in different ways from one another,
your Pisa to my Suurhusen,
until the space between reached
the extreme of square law, inversed.
But did you know there are towers
separately leaning together (Bologna)?
I know it is too late (isn't it?),
but tilting from similar ground
I could whisper over the drop between us
words in my best Italian for building bridges.

Christopher Middleton
The Gnats

Surely our lawn will please the monkey-ghost.
Not in this epoch of epochs only
did more and more come to be forgotten.

Our monkey-ghost treads on the lawn nimbly.
Earth grows crusts that crack and clash,
the river carries grannies and good loam away.

Next thing our monkey-ghost dreams in a hammock.
How sweet our moonlight pulls on a velvet glove.
Would that Vega were conspicuous overhead.

Watching for Vega our monkey-ghost thirsts,
she will not forget the lemon-scented beverage,
but whatever she'd forgotten we forgot it.

Oh, I mean how serious our monkey-ghost is to us,
an hour to go and we are temporarily revised.
Watch well, never let her run foul of the dark.

Show us the horse that does not shudder
catching a whiff of us. Hear our voice,
one and all, drown the growl of the jaguar.

Let us refresh ourself like our monkey-ghost
in depths and varieties of dear life; in the fervour,
the begonia, the badger warren, let us ingest

ichor as yet untasted which toughens its construct,
and always did so while lucidity lasted.
Let our monkey-ghost share with us her lawn.

A A Marcoff
land, & the river

the flower
changes aspect
with the day –
through changing skies & cogencies –
(the shifting of indigo to blue
into violet drift through cloud):
there is a time for petal & colour
to coincide, spring up, & be – lit by a white sun:
it comes as quality, the light,
on deep leaf & ground:
the flower gravitates towards it,
& the sun's bloom & echo come
as waves of light in space: this is God,
this is pure being: see the way
the river cuts through land between the meadows:
it is like steel, but curving,
a collect of shimmer & silk & collage
in which sunrise gathers
its collaborations,
its citrus
potency:

I can touch the flower, forever of now –
this moment of light & petal, clear
with circumstance: the sun is kinetic,
a dawning raw mosaic, calescent:
the river moves towards its end,
water to water, flow to flow:
it is coactive, & conditions the land:
I see a swan search for the sun & fly –
white into light: I see a kingfisher,
distant, down-stream, flash along the surface,
skim the vital air, assertive,
fleeting, wild, then curve
& lift up so suddenly –
brief brilliant
blue

Estill Pollock
At The Window, Last Night's Words, Ashen

At the window, last night's words, ashen
Against the glass

Black petals in the vase, delicate
As the hour fading from us

Their deep scent stirs us
From deeper dreams

Sleepwalkers, we remember
Not knowing the restlessness will pass

What the mouth said
Before it filled with ash

Somewhere in the room, dawn, its thin light
Whining, already awake

David Tait
On Being Trapped Inside A Puddle

In here, among the orange warm
candles to make us romantic. *What is desire?*
Monks look like little flames: on the move
to love and be loved and be fed,
desire to be good, to make merit
into the raised bowl. (*And his arms*
among the din of traffic.) A man puts rice
before our words. We're lost,
you begin but stop. We've said this.
A memory of fire. *What is desire?*
of bowls the monks are carrying, the rim
and every highrise apartment? It's the dull tin
to the sun. We can't see smog
brightening our hangover, adding sun. Rise:
the monks are out on alms again.

The monks are out on alms again
brightening our hangover, adding sunrise
to the sun we can't see. Smog,
and every high rise apartment is the dull tin
of bowls the monks are carrying, the rim
a memory of fire. *What is desire?*
you begin, but stop. We've said this
before. Our words were lost
among the din of traffic. A man puts rice
in the raised bowl and his arms desire
to be good, to make merit,
to love and be loved and be fed.
Monks look like little flames on the move,
candles to make us romantic. What is desire
in here among the orange warm?

Sam Riviere
My Face Saw Her Magazine

across the moonscapes of skateparks you are 13 yrs old
& no longer allowed to play with boys / on platform 6
wearing your amazing cape you are not in fact you
but someone else / while I'm a guy who mishears lyrics
resulting in a more beautiful but private understanding
with your dark fringe white shirt & straw hat you are
the palest goth at the picnic / resolutely uncharmed
by my very charming friend you are the poster of disinterest
in bed & matching underwear you are disguising the tunnel
we dug in the american prison / not answering my texts
what you are is a briefcase glowing with golden contents
I realise I can only look in one eye at a time / it is pure
propaganda the pupil a blot of blackest inkjet ink
in your luxury woollen garment you are an advertisement
for luxury woollen garments / & then & then you wink

POETRY REVIEW WINTER LAUNCH

Everything In Its Season

WITH FLEUR ADCOCK & SAM RIVIERE

Join us in celebrating the launch of the winter issue of *Poetry Review* '*Everything In Its Season*' with **Fleur Adcock** and **Sam Riviere**.

Wednesday 18 January 2012
6.30pm. Readings from 7pm

The Swedenborg Society
20-21 Bloomsbury Way
London WC1A 2TH

TICKETS
£8 Full price
£6 Concessions
£4 PS members

THE POETRY SOCIETY

Tickets from the Poetry Society website at **www.poetrysociety.org.uk**

Telephone bookings: 020 7420 9880
Administration fee charged on telephone bookings

CENTREFOLD

Travelling was where we began.

– Ruth Padel

On Being Old
The Poetry Society Annual Lecture

C.K. WILLIAMS

A novelist friend of mine published an essay a few years ago called 'On Being Beautiful'. I was inspired by her to try a similar title, one which might hearten me to be as frank as she was. Although a few readers grumbled about the possible vanity implied in my friend's words, she is indeed beautiful, as I am indeed old.

I remember the first time I was referred to in print as a "young poet": it happened just about the time I thought I'd moved into early middle age. For some reason poets continue to be called young for a both gratifyingly and irritatingly long time, then you're not anything in particular, and finally you're referred to as... Well, like me, old, or worse, elderly, a word which seems to have lurking in it various cruel decrepitudes. So I'll begin by confessing that the hardest part of being old is admitting to yourself you actually are. That sounds more aphoristic than I mean it to be: the truth is it's a duel, a savage battle. Ten or a hundred times a day sirens wail to remind you that for a minute or two you may have forgotten you're seventy-something, and that you'd better face the fact more realistically. Except there are no instructions as to how to do this: you just know you're kidding yourself if you slip into the benign indifference to passing time we're allowed to enjoy most of our lives.

The rest of aging, at least so far, isn't as bad as it might be. My body hangs together pretty well – the only time it's a bother is when I happen to catch sight of myself in a mirror, especially late at night after too much sight-clearing wine. The upsetting thing then is how in its softenings and sags the body looks simply *stupid*. It doesn't understand the way it once did how important a personage it's lugging around, otherwise it wouldn't dare appear in this gnarled disguise.

It occurs to me to wonder how some of my poet heroes would have looked undressed when they were old. One of the ones I most admire, Robert Frost, I actually met when I was twenty and he was eighty-three. I had a little fling with his granddaughter, and had the chance to spend some time with him. I was so awed that I had no idea what to say to him; I just watched. Physically, by then his face was like a sculpture of itself: something in the public rather than the private realm. His granddaughter I might add was my first critic. I'd just begun to write, and had never shown a poem to anyone but a few non-poet friends. She'd read a lot of poetry, and when I read a poem to her, the second I'd ever written, she said, "That's awful," and I knew she was right.

Which is another thing about looking back from so far: wondering how it all happened to happen. I remember the first time I wrote a reasonably successful poem, but not what I'd had to learn in order to write it. I had an inspiring teacher in college, Morse Peckham, who was then just writing a book on the close reading of poetry, and I learned at least how to read a poem from him, if not how to write one. I also got to know the great architect Louis Kahn quite well: he was a fanatical worker, and I took from him how dedicated you had to be to your art. A little later I came to meet some poets around my age, who taught me a lot, but it still remains a genuine mystery to me how I ever spun a competent poem out of so much snarl.

But I was speaking of the time before all that, when I was subjected to Frost's granddaughter's painful appraisal. I survived that, and worse over the years, but one of the benefits of having lived this long in poetry is that one comes, gratefully, to feel quite distant from the theatrics of criticism. Even if I might still squirm a bit from jabs at my work, I've attained a certain equanimity; except, I should add, when it's clear that a critic hasn't read my poems carefully, or at all. That can happen surprisingly often, and still makes my teeth grind. Mostly, though, it's hard not to perceive how sheerly absurd the stance is of many critics, the way they assume they're more intimate with the genre about which they're commenting than mere practitioners. Certainly critics "know" things, sometimes quite well, but the conviction some have that what they know is more germane to the production of poetry than the poet is can be irksome, to say the least. This is almost never the case when poets write criticism. The greatest poet-critics, like Auden, Heaney, Mandelstam, and Brodsky, always inform their considerations with an awareness of how difficult is the accomplishing of poetry, and how hard it is even to think fruitfully about it.

Young poets, on the other hand, can be pretty obnoxious about it all. The poet-friends I mentioned above – one of whom had already at eighteen published a book, which woefully intimidated me – had a sincere passion to protect the world from what they considered bad poems. *Danger!* they'd cry. *Don't even look! You might turn to poetry stone!* I never could share their fervour and contempt, not because of anything I can call generosity, but because I didn't have the confidence to be that certain about anything. I still mostly don't – I've become over the years more and more conscious of the vagaries of taste.

How shifty a thing taste can be, how shitty, even one's own. I tremble to remember the poets, like Elizabeth Bishop, I dismissed out of hand, whose greatness dawned on me only later. Then there are poets I once admired, and who opened ways through thickets for me, but whose work I now find clumsy and shiftless. I think we all tend to believe we can see through the vagaries of our moment to some absolute standard of judgment – this must be a characteristic of human consciousness itself – but the conviction is absurd. So, I never blab anymore about poets whose work doesn't or no longer moves me, but there are, on the other hand, thank goodness, poets the power and force of whose work once nearly knocked me down me with delight and envy, and still does, so that when I read them again I feel again like an apprentice. About whom here's a poem:

Whacked

Every morning of my life I sit at my desk getting whacked by some
        great poet or other.
Some Yeats, some Auden, some Herbert or Larkin, and lately a
        whole tribe of others—
oi!—younger than me. *Whack!* Wiped out, every day... I mean since
        becoming a poet.
I mean wanting to—one never is, really, a poet. Or I'm not. Not when
        I'm trying to write,
though then comes a line, maybe another, but still pops up again
        Yeats, say, and again *whacked.*

...Wait... Old brain in my head I'd forgotten that "whacked" in crime
        movies means murdered,
rubbed out, by the mob—little the mob-guys would think that poets
        could do it, and who'd believe
that instead of running away you'd find yourself fleeing *towards*
        them, some sweet-seeming Bishop
who's saying SO-SO-SO, but *whack!* you're stampeding again through
        her poems like a mustang,
whacked so hard that you bash the already broken crown of your
        head on the roof of your stall.

...What a relief to read for awhile some bad poems. Still, I try not to
        bad—whackless poems
can hurt you, can say you're all right when you're not, can
        condone your poet-coward
who compulsively asks if you're all right—*Am I all right?*—not
        wasting your time—
Am I wasting time?—though you know you are, wasting time,
        if you're not being *whacked.*
Bad poems let you off that: the confessional mode now: I've
        read reams, I've written as many.

Meanwhile, this morning, this very moment, I'm thinking of
        George Herbert composing;
I see him, by himself, in some candlelit chamber unbearably
        lonely to us but glorious to him,
and he's hunched over, scribbling, scribbling, and the room's
        filling with poems whacking at me,
and Herbert's not even paying attention as the huge tide of them
        rises and engulfs me
in warm tangles of musical down as from the breasts of the
        choiring dawn-tangling larks.

"Lovely enchanting language, sugar-cane…" Whack! *"The sweet
        strains, the lullings..."*
Oh whack! Lowell or Keats, Rilke or Wordsworth or Wyatt:
        whack—fifty years of it,
old race-horse, plug hauling its junk—isn't it time to be put
        out to pasture? But ah, I'd still
if I could lie down like a mare giving birth, arm in my own
        uterine channel to tug out another,
one more, only one more, poor damp little poem, then I'll be
        happy—I promise, I swear.

It's not only one's taste that changes over the course of one's life. In the
early years of my literary education at university and just after, there was a
vogue for myth, folklore, primitive religion, pre-literate song – *The Golden
Bough, The White Goddess, Technicians of the Sacred*: all that. The poets and
intellectuals I knew then weren't much interested in history, or only in so far

as it manifested in poetry and art. Wars, revolutions, social movements, evolving or regressive, all were peripheral to the seriousness of what we thought of as our larger interests. Looking back now, I see those thankfully-few years as a distraction from the real world in which I was living. Because about then in America the Civil Rights Movement dawned, then the Vietnam War was launched, and though such historical upheavals could be enriched by thinking of them in a context of collective unconscious and all that, you could no longer pretend to think seriously about or write about the world without a knowledge of society and history, real history.

Of course, one's own life takes place in history, and generates a history of its own. For a poet, this can be difficult. It's very hard to grasp realistically the trajectory of your own writing life in relation to the world around you, mostly because you've been so preoccupied with the daily, monthly, decadely obsession of writing poems. And then there are times these days when the niggling question surfaces of whether one might actually have written enough poems.

In a sympathetic and intelligent review (the second word devolves directly from the first) of my last book, the poet-critic ended his otherwise favorable observations by remarking that he found the book a third too long. Of course I disagreed, and besides, how many books are there about which something similar couldn't have been said? But still, I wondered whether there might be a model the writer had in mind that my book had violated. And, even more discomfiting: if there's a model for how long a book of poetry should be, might there be a template for a career in poetry? Is there, as the insurance companies in America put it about medical expenses, a life-time limit on the number of poems one is allowed to write?

Then there's that old expression, "something to say." Might one come to a time when indeed one might have nothing more to say? On the other hand, did one ever really start a poem with something to say? Long ago, William Carlos Williams published a book called *I Wanted To Write A Poem*, and before Williams became one of my masters I despised its title, so much so that I wouldn't read the book. In the muddle of my misguided ideals, I believed you weren't supposed just to want to write a poem: poems were meant to germinate from and enact some urgent philosophical or spiritual intuition – their actual composition was somehow incidental to that larger purpose.

I don't know how long it took me – I suppose fortunately not all that long – to grasp that writing a poem, *writing a poem*, was what everything was about. To be a poet isn't to distill ideas, however grand, into verse-language: rather, in the simplest terms, to write poetry is to *sing*. And the task of the poet is to learn to sing, then to do it, then learn it again, and do it a little differently... Of course you do realize as you go along that the song is most compelling when it embodies issues beyond poetry that are crucial to you, and perhaps to others.

The question of whether I might be inflicting poems on the world, though, is less trying than convincing myself that it's worth the effort to write another poem. Writing poems is hard work; not writing them is even harder; no wonder one comes to think: Why bother? Why am I doing this? Then: what have I done with my life? *Written poems?* Written poems when there was so much to be done in the world that needed greater doing? But wait, isn't this the abiding question of lyric poetry, the poetry of an "I"? Who am I thinking about temporality, mortality, beauty or death? Who am I, falling in love? Who am I wandering through the world with nothing much to do, like Whitman, whose work shows you can make yourself and the world and other people monumental by strolling around without much to do?

But in the worst moments, this doesn't relieve the galling sense of repetitiveness and futility. Sometimes it's easier to convince myself to keep at it by thinking of painters or musicians who just seem to do what they do with no fuss. Monet in his hoary old age tottering out to his garden or pond to do one more painting. Or Titian in his ancientness still working. That's what you *do*, that's all. You paint another painting. Or if you're a musician you write another sonata, or symphony, or whatever. The Japanese painter and print maker we know as Hokusai gave himself thirty different names during his life-time. In his seventies he referred to himself as "The old man mad about art" – that's heartening: I like that. It was also around then that he projected a life for himself in which at a hundred he would finally learn how really to paint, and then, he said, at a hundred and thirty "every dot and stroke I paint will be alive." He died at eighty-nine.

In my daily life, though, none of this woolgathering is very useful in revealing what my next poem will be. Yeats wrote, in 'The Circus Animals' Desertion', "I sought a theme, and sought for it in vain…" And that's it exactly. It used to be that "themes" came tumbling from all directions, you just had to get out of the way. But now…

And what makes it even pricklier is how quickly I can fall into a funk when nothing is happening at my desk. This isn't anything new: my editor, who's also a good friend, tells me I've been complaining in much the same way for the nearly forty years we've known each other. Lately, though, I think I've figured out where my desperation comes from.

I used to believe what I thought was a metaphor about writing poetry:

that it's addictive, like a drug. But I understand now that composing verse is actually, not metaphorically, addictive: there really is a kind of *rush*, to use the addicts' term, when you're generating or revising a poem. Busy the mind is, scurrying this way and that, spinning and soaring, and, as is apparently the case with stimulants, there's an altered experience of time, and of the self as it moves through time – I'm sure other poets know what I mean by this. And they must know too that when one isn't working on a poem, doesn't have any poetry work to do, there are real withdrawal symptoms. In my case, I fall into something like depression, and as in other depressions, I begin to doubt, to ask questions I shouldn't, about my work, my life – all I grumbled about just now. Goethe put it succinctly: "The poet's requisite trance is the most fragile element in his armoury."

The other realization I've had recently was that some of this paradoxically has to do with the years I've practiced my craft. I'm more efficient now when I work; it doesn't take me as long to make decisions about a poem, to revise or reconceive it. This is all well and good, and I certainly won't complain, except that my proficiency leaves me with more time on my hands to suffer the absence of the excitement of poetry labour. I sit and stare, I close my eyes, I read other people's poems or don't, it doesn't matter. Of course reading great poems, especially for the first time, has its own addictive thrill – it's almost as good as going at one's own work – but there aren't all that many great poems which after all these decades haven't already found me. So it can be a relief when a friend sends me a poem to make suggestions about – at least I'm *doing something*.

One thing that does keep me going in the end is change, the sound of my poems changing, their tone, voice, velocity, general shape. Knowing how or why these changes come about I've always found impossible to describe: they just happen, and I tag along. After my most recent book, *Wait*, I found myself writing poems unlike any I'd written before. There seemed to have arrived in them an element not only of the irrational, but the absurd, a willed goofiness that for some reason pleases me. 'Whacked' is an example of this. Maybe I'm tired of being logical, rational, lucid, "mature". I knew all along I was never any of these things: sanity was always a kind of armour I donned before I went into the fray of composition – and of life, too, I suppose. When I hit seventy or so, it came to me that I hadn't changed a bit since I was eighteen – Yeats once said something similar – or even since I was twelve. I often feel as chartless as I was then, meandering through the world without much definite sense of direction. As a kid that was mostly okay, until the tornado of adolescence whirled me into the mind I had to live with for the next fifty years, when I finally landed where occasionally I can relax and be myself again.

"Being oneself." Isn't that the most absurd phrase? As though there's a choice? In the life of art, though, every day can feel like a choice. Who am I today? Am I a *poet* today, one who might write a poem? Or am I that clod who dared cultivate the desire to string words together in a *poetic* way? So, again: will I finally be myself today? Or is the myself today the same poet who wrote with certain musicks until now, and will I have to write in those musicks, which may by now be utterly tedious, again?

It may well be that the self I am today just doesn't want to make the same damned noise. Maybe that noise has become boring. How do I change it? Do I invent a different poet? Do I study the music of different poets from those I've known? Don't I know them all? Besides, if the poems do change, as I say mine recently have, is it really because of some choice? Have I ever *chosen* the music of a particular poem? Isn't it always rather that the music of the poems seems to choose *me*? Which me? A choiceless choice.

All right: after all the poetry business, how can an old man speak of life without coming sooner or later to death? Dear death, our faithful lifelong companion. But before I consider death itself, it would be cowardly not to confront the worse than death. I mean the other, more dreadful fates that lurk in one's quickly diminishing future: the horror shows of dementia, amnesia, aphasia, even the mostly unremarkable memory loss, the last of which already afflicts me, leaving me occasionally stricken with embarrassment before people I know well whose name all at once isn't there.

The worst of these soul-killers, Alzheimer's and its kin, many of us who work with our minds believe are worse than merely dying. It would be pleasant to be amusing here, to find a tone sufficiently flip to distance myself from the terrible implications of this, the way Philip Larkin did it in 'The Old Fools'. That's a terrifying poem, where old age is characterized finally as "The whole hideous inverted childhood", but in which Larkin still managed to employ his inimitable tone of detachment, irony, self-mocking; stances I find to be utterly beyond me. My own poem about these matters I suppose has quite a bit less detachment:

Rat Wheel, Dementia, Mont Saint Michel

for Albert O. Hirschman

My last god's a theodicy glutton, a good-evil gourmet—
peacock and plague, gene-junk; he gobbles it down.
Poetry, violence; love, war—his stew of honey and thorn.

For instance, thinks theodicy-god: Mont Saint Michel.
Sheep, sand, steeple honed sharp as a spear. And inside,
a contraption he calls with a chuckle the rat-wheel.

Thick timber three meters around, two persons across,
into which prisoners were inserted to trudge, toil,
hoist food for the bishop and monks; fat bishop himself.

The wheel weighs and weighs. You're chained in; you toil.
Then they extract you. Where have your years vanished?
What difference? says theodicy-god. Wheel, toil: what difference?

Theodicy-god has evolved now to both substance and not.
With handy metaphysical blades to slice brain meat from mind.
For in minds should be voidy wings choiring, not selves.

This old scholar, for instance, should have to struggle to speak,
should not remember his words, paragraphs, books:
that garner of full-ripened grain must be hosed clean.

Sometimes as the rat-wheel is screaming, theodicy-god
considers whether to say he's sorry: That you can't speak,
can't remember your words, paragraphs, books.

Sorry, so sorry. Blah, his voice thinks instead, blah.
He can't do it. Best hope instead they'll ask him again
as they always do for forgiveness. But what if they don't?

What might have once been a heart feels pity, for itself though,
not the old man with no speech—for him and his only scorn.
Here in my rat wheel, my Mont Saint Michel, my steeple of scorn.

But then, again, after everything, death. How death shape-changes over the decades. My own most intimate relationship to death occurred in my twenties. Death then was with me all the time, as a threat, and also, as I've said, a companion, a possible saviour, but in whatever guise it took, it was *there*. I remember thinking at one point that the most appropriate title for my first book of poems, the book I never finished writing, should have been *The Book of Dying*.

It's different now. Death only takes me occasionally these days, and doesn't hang about the way it did then. It comes instead in sudden, dire surges, in which everything is infused with death, flooded away. During those times, usually at dawn when I wake too early, death possesses reality, not as fear, but fact, inevitable, unavoidable, complete. And along with this, or just subsequent to it, I'm jettisoned into time in an unfamiliar way. In that early light, I often find myself ranging restlessly over my past as I never used to. I'm back in my twenties or thirties or even before, taken by spookily animated memories. All the thoughtless and stupid things I said, years ago, decades ago, I find have been dutifully stored in some cesspool of conscience that only now has taken to overflowing, so that my selfishness, my awful insensitivity, all which at the time I thought were a portion of how one was in the world, return with distressing clarity.

The journeys I make through time aren't only in my own life, though. I also find myself traveling through larger cycles as well. I refer a lot in my mind to the far past, to history, and even to pre-homo-sapiens existence. I keep trying to give credence to the fact that my own personal ancestors were these hairier other humans, the possible lives of which I find so engrossing.

Then, again, more often, I find myself spun out into the future. I obsess about the future much more than I ever did before, much more than I'd like to. What terrible possibilities await us, or, more poignantly and painfully, our heirs. I remember the first time I heard the term "global warming". I felt a chill: it was clear that we, all of us, were involved in a destiny much larger than any we'd ever imagined. The survival of the planet as we know it was going to be our responsibility. These days I think a lot about this, I dwell on its terribly plausibility. Sometimes I can't think about anything else – I find myself too often writing mostly wretched poems about it.

Galway Kinnell has a poem, 'There Are Things I Tell To No One'. A lovely title, to which in my memory I'd found I'd added a phrase, "but the poem." Except I find now that there is indeed much, very much, I not only don't tell the poem, but don't tell anyone else either. I have a wife I love unreasonably, a son and a daughter, three grandsons and a son-in-law, and many beloved friends. I worry about them, and I don't want to tell those closest to me how dire my vision of the future is, for fear of terrifying them. I'm not bringing any news to them, surely, but they respect what I think, and feel, and I'm afraid my anxieties will only intensify their own. There are times I'm almost relieved that I won't have to live to see the worst of it, and others when I almost wish not to perceive what's out there right now. Trying to save our world has become, in America at least, a partisan political issue, contaminated by the cynical cultivation by the Right of willful superstition. I find this to be the most atrocious example of corruption that we've had to behold in our already harrowing historical moment.

The rest of our communal madness goes on, as usual. Watching the news, realizing again how such and such number of people had been killed in one country then another, I wonder how many times in our media-saturated culture we hear that word "killed" spoken, and how difficult it still is to grasp the reality that each occasion represents a person with a consciousness of the mysteries of existence exactly like our own, which will no longer be an consciousness, but a void. Horrible thought.

And in its way a childish one. Children think like that, one thing at a time. It takes us a long time to learn to abstract from the instance. But not that long. When he was three, my grandson Sully asked his mother, "When you step on an ant, does it say 'ouch?'" "Ants don't talk," my daughter answered. "Yes," Sully said, " but does it say 'ouch' in its mind?"

We come to know this thing called mind quite early on, and we also at some point much later come to realize how much our minds aren't susceptible to being what we'd like them to be. As I've aged – *matured* I suppose would be the word – I've become more and more aware of the parts of myself that don't arrive at anything like what's implied by that grand term. The older I am, the more I've become aware of how trapped I am in a mind that in its perceptions, its impulses, its emotions, is very much still a child's. I've spent so much time, so much labour, trying to tame this thing called mind, trying to cajole it to be more reasonable, more sensible, less absolute, less simply silly. But the task seems hopeless, because my child's mind, the mind that lurks beneath all the others I like to think determine who I am, experiences the world in brute, crude, utterly unsophisticated systems of feeling and thought: it wants, it wishes, it desires – things, feelings, states of being – and when it isn't granted them to possess, or at least hope for, it becomes depressed, or flies into a tantrum. And, worse, it's not satisfied with halfways: it admits no partials, no gradations, no compromises or concessions; to it accommodations are capitulations, failures, precursors to defeat.

Furthermore, that the world beyond me is not as my child's mind wishes it to be, imagines it can be, is passionately convinced it absolutely *should* be, throws it into a frenzy of frustration, exasperation, indignation, umbrage, so that I, trapped for so much of the time in this my mind, am offended, embittered; I disapprove, I sulk, I become petulant. When I look out into that world, when I peer out between my petulance and my sulk at that world which at once lacks, and is in danger – how can it not be that I am fraught? How can my mind not be frightened not only of the world, but also of itself, this child's mind which inflicts the imperfect world on itself?

But then, sooner or later, again and again, I ask myself how can the world's ultimate facticity, the simplicity of it, its purity, not be dimmed, diminished, thrown out of focus, distorted by a surrender to myself, by my helplessness before myself? I see the world as it is, its space, its people, its things; I see it glowing in the astonishment of pure being, yet the emotion I draw from that glow, from that blaze, is worry, concern, anguish; is anxiety, terror, then sadness, then, again, despair, that despair which seems not merely to perceive the world beyond itself, but in its imagination to consume it.

And so I mostly shut up about my despair. Sometimes perhaps telling a poem, but mostly struggling to keep it to myself.

As I will here. And return to death, which, in this context, can sometimes be, as I've said, solacing. Not to have to behold the rains stop, the deserts advance, the glaciers melt, and to experience the violence and suffering that may well ensue from such disruptions.

And yet reality, our reality, is here, it beckons, it hasn't lost a bit of its glorious clarity, its colours, its sounds, its scents, those simple miracles which are more miraculous in the complexities science has revealed woven beneath them. I desire this world with the unquestioning, unconditional force of a love that forever wends a way through the interstices of disappointment, dissatisfaction, foreboding.

And poetry. It doesn't seem absurd after all to have given one's life to poetry. To have been allowed to participate in the grandeur of its traditions, to have experienced so profoundly so many inspiring poems, so many poet-geniuses, so many glimmers of something greater than anything I could have imagined life would offer, life would be. Even unto death, poetry can go on, will go on.

Writers Writing Dying

Many I could name but won't who'd have been furious to die
                      while they were sleeping but did—
outrageous, they'd have lamented, and never forgiven the
                      death they'd construed for themselves
being stolen from them so rudely, so crudely, without feeling
                      themselves like rubber gloves
stickily stripped from the innermostness they'd contrived to
                      horde for so long—all of it gone,
squandered, wasted, on what? *Death*, crashingly boring as long
                      as you're able to think and write it.

Think, write, write, think: just keep galloping faster and you
                      won't even notice you're dead.
The hard thing's when you're not thinking or writing and as
                      far as you know you are dead
or might as well be, with no word for yourself, just that
                      suction shush like a heart pump or straw
in a milkshake and death which once wanted only to be sung
                      back to sleep with its tired old fangs
has me in its mouth!— and where the hell are you that chunk
                      of dying we used to call Muse?

Well, dead or not, at least there was that dream, of some
                      scribbler, some think- and write- person,
maybe it was yourself, soaring in the sidereal void, and not
                      only that, you were holding a banjo
and gleefully strumming, and singing, jaw swung a bit under
                      and off to the side the way crazily
happily people will do it—singing songs or not even songs, just
                      lolly molly syllable sounds
and you'd escaped even from language, from having to gab,
                      from having to write down the idiot gab.

But in the meantime isn't this what it is to be dead, with that
        Emily-fly buzzing over your snout
that you're singing almost as she did; so what matter if you
        died in your sleep, or rushed toward dying
like the Sylvia-Hart part of the tribe who ceased too quickly to
        be and left out some stanzas?
So what? You're still aloft with your banjoless banjo, and if
        you're dead or asleep who really cares?
Such fun to wake up though! Such fun too if you don't! Keep
        dying! Keep writing it down!

C.K. Williams has won the National Book Critics Circle Award, a Pulitzer Prize, the Los Angeles Times Book Prize, the National Book Award and the Ruth Lilly Poetry Prize. He teaches at Princeton University.

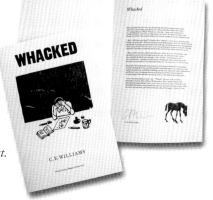

THE SEASONAL WORLD

The Season Of The Newts

RICHARD KERRIDGE

I didn't think I would see any. The pond was drab, empty. Reeds were still brown from winter. Crinkled leaves floated. It was too early in the year, and too cold. I walked around the pond. Beetles darted here and there. A leech lengthened and contracted like an elephant's trunk. Something about two sticks on the bottom, one across the other, made me look again. Thick little, muddy black sticks – but I saw it now, the line of crest running down each back, the blunt heads, transparent jelly round the eyes. Even the feet in the mud were clear now, with the toes ringed in yellow. Two male Great Crested Newts, motionless.

I crouched and leaned forward. A puff of mud and they were gone.

When I was a boy I hunted them fruitlessly. We all caught Smooth Newts in the park ponds. There were rumours of Great Cresteds. In the playground, Tony Luffingham boasted that he could get them, but never brought any. Someone talked about a pond down in Sussex, and we cycled out of London with vague directions. Near Uckfield, they said. We found a pond, perhaps the right one, and waded about until it was muddy soup and we had dragged every clump of weed onto the bank. Silently we picked through the weed. A dark female Smooth, fat and squashy, was caught in the weed; it was a noose round her body, too tight. I eased the loop over her head. She was the biggest Smooth I'd ever seen, plump with eggs. In my fingers she flapped like a fish. We said she was a Crested, but she wasn't.

I'd seen the illustrations. They were the biggest newts, black as fresh tar. An old book from the library called them The Great Crested or Warty Newt, or just The Warty Newt, for their skins were a surface of pimples, black caviar. Their golden eyes gleamed. I never saw one.

Sometimes I thought I'd glimpsed one, in the middle, in the great ravines of chokeweed.

But today I'd seen two. After dark I went back. Spots of rain pricked my cheeks. My beam on the weed found a toad: loose bag of a body, emptied of spawn, looking up. It tipped forward, swam jerkily, butting the bank. Small newts hung in the water.

There was a white shape over there, a carrier bag billowing, and next to it a male Great Crested in full display, arching his back. He twisted and corkscrewed, flashing his belly, yolk yellow blotched in black. The female walked towards him. Large and deliberate, she pushed past. He swam round to face her, high crest quivering. She pushed past again. He went into a paroxysm, painfully arched and twisting, over her head, and down with his nose to hers, body lifting. He let it lift. His tail went up, and body, and he was dancing vertically, nose down, writhing coil of black and yellow. She was still. His eyes were mad like a bull's.

Another male moved up next to him, smaller. As he turned, I saw that a leg was missing. Or, at least, the flesh. White and stiff, like an ivory toothpick, the bone jutted out. Something had pulled off all the tissue like a glove.

The female moved on.

For most of the year they live out of the water and tighten into drab, slow, rubbery lumps. Dust sticks to their bodies. The crests have gone. But in spring, in the ponds, those bodies soften and open out, like paper in water, or sea anemones when the tide returns. The males start to dance, their crests flaming. What does it feel like, that loosening and frenzy? What do the females see, when this mad, bright creature coils twisting in front of them? They dance at night. The whole pond is darkness. Something must seep in through her porous skin, her froth of skin, softening her, filling her.

I switched off my torch. I had rain in my hair. A car went past. Houses were all around. Did people here know about these newts? Did they throng the banks when the season started, crisscrossing the pond with their torchlights, whispering and pointing? Why didn't they? It could be like the cranes in Nebraska.

Back at my car, under a streetlamp, something on the ground caught my eye. A female was poised on the edge of the kerb, gazing out like a gargoyle, flexing her toes, sensing the pond, tense at the huge things around her. My foot was inches away. What could her eyes and skin do with these lights and cruel tarmac? Once I would have gasped at this find. I carried her to the pond, cold in my hand, and to drop her in turned on my torch. The male was still dancing.

Richard Kerridge has twice won the *BBC Wildlife* Award for Nature Writing.

from The Mara Crossing

RUTH PADEL

You really feel the earth turn in September. The planet is sliding us into autumn. On the other side of the Equator it must be sliding everyone into spring but here every morning seems a little darker.

I come into the kitchen and see starlings round the bird feeders outside. Dawn glows through the geisha fans of their wings as they try to eat and flutter at the same time. One of them does it by hanging upside-down and sticking its tail over its head. They may live in London the whole year but they could have flown across the English Channel last night.

Starlings are partial migrants – some migrate, some don't. Huge flocks arrive every autumn on England's east coast and radiate out to join other starlings across the country. In spring, hundreds of thousands go back to nest in Eastern Europe.

*

We were all wanderers once. We walked out of Africa looking for food, safety, water, shelter and territory. Travelling was where we began and *homo viator*, man the pilgrim, life as pilgrimage, is deep-engrained in Western thought. Mediaeval Christianity said we were strangers in this world, searching for the spiritual homeland to which we originally belonged. We weren't meant to be here – we were put in a garden. But that went wrong; now we are wanderers between two worlds, wayfarers on the *via*, the 'way', of life; both fixed and wandering, settlers and nomads. Our history is the story of the nomad giving way to the settler but when people are unsettled they have to migrate. The point of migration, whether you are a starling or a human being, is to reach whatever helps you and your children live in a new place.

Home and migration belong together, two sides of the same ancient coin. Home is something we make, then things change either in ourselves or in the world, we lose home and have to go elsewhere.

The word 'migrate' covers many sorts of move. It comes from Latin *migrare*, 'to move from one place to another' and is related to 'mutable' and Greek *ameibein*, 'to change'. We mainly use it for two types of journey. Both can be undertaken either by large groups or individuals. The two have a lot in common, but there is a wide spectrum between. The type of migration we think of in relation to animals, a periodic and usually seasonal move from one place to another and back, I shall call Go and Come Back. Human migrant workers and commuters do it too. The other type, Go and Stay, is a permanent move to a new region and often overlaps invasion and colonization. We might think of it as typically human but animals and plants do it too. Only humans, however, go in for emigration (going permanently away from home) or immigration (coming to settle permanently in a new home). These words suggest a political boundary has been crossed.

Another word to throw into the mix, sometimes used interchangeably with migration, is transmigration. It can mean moving from one place, or one stage of life, to another. But it has the extra dimension of reincarnation: the soul is moving to another body to be born again. Underneath all this is the idea of travelling towards something you need and don't have. There is a push factor and and a pull factor. The push may be escaping war, or famine, or a freezing winter. The pull is usually safety, warmth, food or work. But whichever is uppermost, whether the travel is cyclical like swallows or once in a lifetime, migration is about survival.

The push factor is both outer and inner. The external forces may be geographical and climatic like an ice age or the arrival of a competing species but there is always an abstract way of putting them: as a loss, danger, or a lack – which triggers inner pressures to which we give other abstract names like hunger, fear or hope and the great dream – of something better elsewhere. In human migration, hope and imagination are push and pull combined. The great positive force behind human migration is hope of a new life.

*

There are now five goldfinches, flakes of flying red and gold flitting through apple boughs above the feeders, waiting for the starlings to leave. They raised a family round here this summer: I have watched the chicks grow the scarlet on their faces.

*

The original migration was the spread of blue-green algae over the globe. A cell makes protein, dismantles it and starts again: that's metabolism, which creates the energy cells need, in order to respond to whatever is around them. The first metabolizing cells emerged from water and set off into the unknown on the adventure of self-replication as if they had heard God say, on the fifth day of creation *Go forth and multiply*. Social studies say human migrants are changed by the new home, the place to which they come, but also change that place, and that is exactly what the first cells did to earth's atmosphere: they oxygenated it. The earth changed. As a result more complex life-forms evolved and spread further.

Five hundred million years ago, proper land plants developed and spread away from the water. A hundred and thirty million years after that, the first tree, Archaeopteris, developed out of them. It grew sixty to ninety feet high and was the first plant to have large spreading roots. Archaeopteris is extinct now, but in the late Devonian era, about 370 million years ago, it spread across the world to create the life-form which made possible our life on earth – the first forest.

Archaeopteris changed the chemistry of the soil and the atmosphere: its roots dug in and its ferny canopy absorbed carbon dioxide. Smaller plants developed, taking more carbon dioxide out of the atmosphere, injecting oxygen in. Carbon dioxide levels sank, land temperatures dropped, animals could move over land without overheating because with less carbon dioxide, the ozone layer above Earth grew and shielded them from ultraviolet radiation. Trees nourished life in water as decaying trunks and leaf litter fed the streams and freshwater fish evolved. Safe from ultraviolet rays, in a milder climate, the new animals ate food provided by the plants or by each other. Grass evolved. New animals evolved to eat it.

Plant migration made earth a place where animals could breathe. Trees and plants are rooted but their migration created the forests: their very existence is a result of movement. Cells migrate in the body but stay safely (otherwise we'd all be in trouble) inside it. Migration is part of the restless, constantly self-renewing nature of all life, in creative tension between the fixed and the wandering.

*

When the starlings fly off, the goldfinches flutter onto the nyger seeds and a blackbird shrills an alarm call from the ancient plum tree.

Our plums are damsons, unusually sweet this year, unusually thick on the bough. Once handled, they change colour for ever: the indigo sheen disappears and you see pink-violet beneath. The tree itself now is almost blue; the plums have pulled the branches low over the grass. My daughter is in London at the moment, working as intern at a foundation that helps asylum-seekers. She collects the blue plums in a yellow bucket.

Trees seem such fixtures, but they were the first great land migrants. Like their ancestor Archaeopteris, modern trees spread over the planet, but as the climate changed, ice appeared and trees migrated away from it. Where there was space, as in North America, trees migrated over mountains and crossed continents. Northern trees migrated south during the Pleistocene age (2,600,000 to 11,700 years ago), when the Laurentide ice sheet covered North America east of the Rockies from the Arctic down to where New York, St. Louis and Kansas City are now. When the world warmed up again, tundra plants re-colonized newly bared soil; then northern trees came back on the heels of the melting ice. 18,000 years ago came spruce and northern pine; several thousand years afterwards came fir and birch.

But in Britain trees had nowhere to escape to. The last Ice Age wiped them out, except for the strawberry tree in south Ireland. When the ice melted, thirty-three species migrated back to Britain from what is now mainland Europe. First the birch and Scots pine, lastly the hornbeam and beech. Then rising sea-levels cut Britain off from Europe, the Channel ended tree migration and Britain was left with those thirty-three, now called our 'native' trees.

But what does 'native' mean? These were post-glacial migrants. The DNA of our most ancient oaks says they came from the Iberian peninsula. That makes the Royal Oak, emblem of England, an immigrant from Spain.

*

Our small garden is stuffed with plants. We have been here fifteen years; my daughter has grown up here as the garden grew shaggier and more jungly. But few of these plants are native. Rhododendrons came from the Himalaya. The damson, like the horse chestnut, came with the Romans, who clearly adored damsons. Archaeologists find the stones while digging up Roman camps. The Romans discovered damsons a hundred years before they colonized Britain, while conquering a much older civilization, Syria. But though the damson was first cultivated in Damascus, the oldest continuously inhabited city in the world, wild damsons go back much further. They evolved where the ancestors of apples began too, in south China.

The apple family, *malus*, probably evolved about twelve million years ago in the mountain system known as Tien Shan, bordering Kazakhstan and Kyrgystan. As these mountains rose, the snow melt created subterranean caves and the bear population exploded. Through millennia, munching and choosing, extending their territory, bears gradually converted the hawthorn berry into the apple and the sloe into the damson and spread them more widely. Fruit trees migrate by a forced migration: the seeds travel in the intestines of animals who drop them, fertilized by dung, in alien soil.

When humans appeared they spread fruit trees further. They found they could store apples through winter, carry them on journeys. The story of the apple is the story of interaction between plants, animals and people whose horses trod pips into the soil of forests and plains.

*

Inside all these bears, apples, horses and humans, other life-forms were evolving and migrating with them. Four billion years ago some genes discovered they could spread by tricking other genes into replicating them. Parasites replicate their DNA with the help of, and at the expense of, someone else's. They existed long before land animals appeared; new ones evolved at every new stage of life's complexity. Flatworms made their way into crustaceans then diversified into flukes and tapeworms.

Parasites drove evolution. Their hosts evolved ways of protecting themselves so parasites adapted to evade the policing and the host had to adapt further to protect itself. The parasites which survived were those that spread into more and better places to live. Today parasites make up most life on earth and outnumber other living species by four to one. Diseases migrated with their hosts. From a parasite's point of view, many symptoms of disease, like coughing, are the clever ways it has found to change our body's behaviour so that it, itself, may multiply and spread.

They do this in thousands of different ways, like the open sores of syphilis, which seems a comparatively new disease. Syphilis has always been seen as the unwelcome immigrant, coming from somebody and somewhere else. France called it the Italian Disease, the Dutch the Spanish Disease, Russians called it the Polish Disease, Turks the Christian or Frank Disease, Tahiti the British Disease. It was spread mainly by sailors but no one knows where it began. Was it a New World disease brought to Europe by Colombus or were Hippocratic doctors already describing it in the fourth century BC? The first well-recorded European outbreak was in 1494 among French troops who may have caught it via Spanish mercenaries while besieging Naples. Then it rampaged across Europe. Before 1530 the Italians, Poles and Germans were already calling it the French Disease.

Malaria, though, is much older. As the Romans brought damsons to Britain, so humans brought malaria out of Africa. China and ancient Egypt knew it 5,000 years ago, India 3,000 years ago, the Mediterranean 2,500 years ago. Human migration spread it to southern Europe, the Arabian peninsula, Asia, northern Europe. In the 15th century, trade and colonization spread it to the New World and South-East Asia through Europe but also via African slaves brought by Spanish colonisers.

Plasmodium, the parasite that causes malaria, is passed on by the female anopheline mosquito, which needs blood to develop her eggs. (Only females bite; males stick to glucose.) The parasite develops in her tiny gut, enters our blood through her saliva and is carried into the liver where it invades cells and multiplies. Then it returns to the blood, penetrates red cells and multiplies further breaking the red cells down.

Today a million and a half people die from it every year. Plasmodium, like hackers, always tries to be ahead of the game: it is developing immunity to chemicals we find to counter it. Every forty-five seconds, says an ad in my newspaper today, another child dies of malaria. Nature's forms do not demonstrate benevolence, said Darwin, divine or otherwise.

In Christianity, the Fall is the story of how something harmful got into the system from the start. (One name for Satan is *alienus*, the stranger, the outsider.) Parasites tell the same story: cells have smaller cells within them which flourish at their expense and accompany them everywhere. We, mosquitoes and plasmodium evolved and spread together.

*

But though migration spreads disease, migration also defends us from it. Atoms migrate in a molecule, teeth migrate in our mouths and cells migrate in our bodies. They move by pushing protrusions out at their front and drawing in their trailing ends. Their migration is the Go and Stay type and happens for two reasons. One is to create new life, as cells migrate in a pregnant mother to form a foetus. The other is to defend us against harm. Cell migration is the basis of the immune system. Cells migrate to a site of infection or trauma, travelling towards wounds to attack invading bacteria. They migrate, in other words, to heal, repair damage and create new life. This is not circulation but the maintenance of our fabric.

"Cells are guided", a cell biologist told me, "by migration-promoting chemicals they detect in their environment. They find some attractive and like to go towards them and find others repulsive and try to get away from them. If you supply the chemical with a needle and move your needle round, the cells chase it."

"Why call it migrating?" I asked.

"To give an impression of purpose," he said. "The cells just seem to be trying to go somewhere. Purposefully."

So is all motivation ultimately chemical? Maybe the answer is that all purpose has some chemical dimension, but, as with the different factors of push and pull behind migration, that doesn't mean there aren't others too. Our own bodies show us that however many purposes there are behind migration, the bottom line is twofold: to heal and to create new life.

*

Bird migration is the heartbeat of the planet. Along ancient routes, nothing to do with human frontiers, millions of birds are weaving the world together all the time. They are migration's blue-print, reminding us that earth and the life it sustains are constantly changing form and changing place. Their migrations, especially, have made them for us an image of hope.

"Hopes are shy birds," wrote John James Audubon in his journal in 1820, "flying at a great distance." Audubon had been focussed on birds since he was young. He had just said goodbye to his beloved wife and children; he was taking a boat down the Ohio River on the first leg of his journey to Britain where he hoped to find someone to print and publish his bird paintings. There, giving a talk in Edinburgh on birds of North America, he would inspire a sixteen-year old medical student whom his family called 'Bobby', who hated the course he was doing just as Audubon had once hated being a naval cadet.

Audubon and that medical student had a couple of things in common. Both had to cope with great loss when they were small and did it by turning to nature – to long solitary walks and bird-watching. Audubon chose birds (or they chose him) as a way to make sense of the world. His mother died when he was little; Charles Darwin's died when he was eight. "Why does every gentleman not become an ornithologist?" Darwin wondered when he was ten. At Edinburgh, instead of attending operations and medical lectures, Darwin took bird-stuffing tutorials from a local taxidermist. Birds are an image of escape from where and what you are right now. "Hope is the thing with feathers," says Emily Dickinson, "That perches in the soul."

*

Recently, after the funeral of one of my uncles, I drove to a family gathering at his home in the Chiltern Hills. Near the house I saw a red kite close up.

There was a flash of hooded amber eyes and then it swooped away. Its shadow crossed a sunlit field while the bird itself was soaring into blue sky. Suddenly cells got muddled up in my mind with what they sounded like – souls.

For millennia we have taken birds as an image of the soul. Death, we have told each other, is the soul doing what birds do, winging its way to a better place; possibly to return. In sorrow for my uncle, I thought of transmigration: souls migrating into a new life, either into a new body or into heaven. The bird, I thought, and the shadow of the bird. The cell and the soul. Those are the boundaries of migration.

This extract is taken from *The Mara Crossing*, forthcoming from Chatto, January 2012. Writer in Residence at the Environment Institute and History Department, University College London, Ruth Padel's most recent book is *Silent Letters of the Alphabet*, Bloodaxe, 2010.

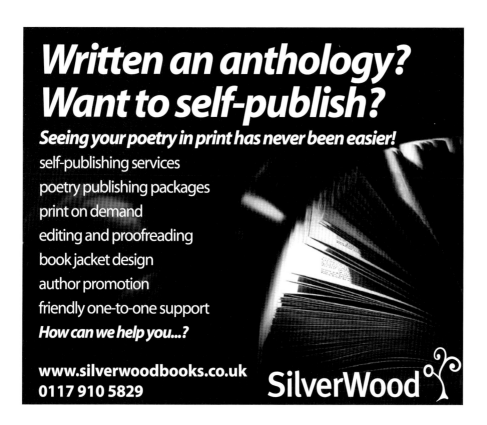

KISS THE WINGED JOY AS IT FLIES

Fleur Adcock
At The Crossing

The tall guy in a green T-shirt,
vanishing past me as I cross
in the opposite direction,
has fairy wings on his shoulders:
toy ones, children's fancy-dress wings,
cartoonish butterfly cut-outs.

Do they say gay? No time for that.
He flickers past the traffic lights –
whoosh! gone! – outside categories.
Do they say foreign? They say young.
They say London. Grab it, they say.
Kiss the winged joy as it flies.

Traffic swings around the corner;
gusts of drizzle sweep us along
the Strand in the glittering dark,
threading to and fro among skeins
of never-quite-colliding blurs.
All this whirling's why we came out.

Those fragile flaps could lift no one.
Perhaps they were ironic wings,
tongue-in-cheek look-at-me tokens
to make it clear he had no need
of hydraulics, being himself
Hermes.
        Wings, though; definite wings.

Blow Flies

If you liked them, how your heart might have lifted
to see their neat trapezium shapes studding
the wall like a newly landed flight of jet
ornaments, the intensity of their black
gloss, with secret blues and greens half-glinting through,
and the glass wings, not so unlike those of bees –

if you could bring yourself; if they occupied
a niche in creation nudged fractionally
sideways –
                          because it's not their present forms, it's
their larval incarnations that you can't stop
heaving into view, white nests moistly seething
in a dead pigeon or a newspaper-wrapped
package leaking beside a path (but enough –
the others will kindly absent themselves, please!)

and wondering what, where – under the floorboards
or behind the freezer – suddenly hatched these.

Bat Soup

But it's diluted with sky, not water,
the aerial plankton on which they sup.
Our solitary pipistrelle flickers
over her chosen suburban quarter,
echo-locating, to siphon it up.
It nourishes birds as well as bats –
high-flyers that feed on the wing,
swifts, house-martins – this floating gruel
of hymenoptera, midges and gnats,
thunderbugs, beetles, aphids, flies,
moths, mosquitoes, and flying dots
almost too small to be worth naming.

Some of it swirls at a lower level –
a broth of midges over a pool
at dusk or a simultaneous hatch
of mayflies boiling up from Lough Neagh:
swallow-fodder, and also a splotch
to plaster on any passing windscreen,
though even at speed there's never so much
as of yore; bad news for the food-chain,
but somehow *'ou sont les neiges d'antan'*
sounds too noble a note of dole
for a sullying mash of blood and chitin.
(And we can't hear what the bats are screaming).

Turkish Poets
Of The Balkans

SELECTED AND TRANSLATED BY MEVLUT CEYLAN

Mevlut Ceylan, Director of the newly-inaugurated Yunus Emre Turkish Cultural Centre in London, selects and translates poetry of the Balkan Turk communities.

These substantial communities are at least in part a legacy of the Ottoman Empire. Bulgaria's half a million Turks make up roughly eight per cent of the population; roughly nine per cent of Bulgarians have Turkish as their mother tongue. In Macedonia, Turks constitute the third largest ethnic group; roughly two hundred thousand Macedonians speak a Macedonian Turkish with Slavic and Greek admixtures. Only about one per cent of Kosovans are Turks; most live and around the town of Prizren and there is another small community in Kosovska Mitrovica.

MACEDONIA

Ilhami Emin
My Sister's Flowers

A bunch of flowers
Smiled from the balcony
Opposite
Understanding that I'm looking at Fahriye Abla

A bunch of flowers
Understanding that I'm looking at
Fahriye Abla
Smiled at me
From the balcony
Opposite

BULGARIA

Fevzi Kadir Sever
As I Live

I didn't know how to lie
I've been deceived many times
I learnt
But I didn't teach anyone
How to lie

I fell in love many times
Every beautiful girl taught me something
Kisses and many more kisses
But I did not humiliate myself

Şükrü Esen
My Village In Rodop

In my dream I was in my village again.
I was in our old house
And I was eight.
I still can remember
          That first step,
My first footstep when I left
When my mother was young
And my brothers and sisters
          Went to the mountains to pick flowers.

Sometimes sadness sometimes happiness
Fill my eyes with tears.
I'm waiting.
My father will come back from abroad,
He'll bring those balloons I asked for
And I'll be happy,

And then
My childhood can
Fly away
Like one of those balloons.

Necmiye Mehmet Ulucan
Vaso Valo

If one day I break
my favourite vase and go
I won't come back
though I'll weep
at the end of a street
where you've gone
looking for me.

If I burn down a house one day
I'll have run away
scared to death
day and night
night and day
and you'll have to took for me
as if I were your brother
lost somewhere in the mountains.

Even if you kill me
one day
and run away to hide
there'll be no need to hide
because I'll find you
and console you.

KOSOVO

Murteza Büşra
Friends

Lokach in Spring
And Divanyolu
And Kuri Ibrahim too –
Oh my dear friends,
My city was so beautiful!

Spring – sublime beauty of life!
Such splendour!
Such coquettishness!

Dear, dear friends,
Are these poems
And all that's happened –
Are they a first spring love?

Nusret Dişo Ülkü
I Like First Things

I've always liked first things:
The sound of the first bell
For the first lesson
With me in the first row.

I've always liked first things:
My first school,
My first class
And my first teacher.

I've always liked first things:
My first text book,
My first exercise book,
My first pen.

I've always liked first things:
The first letter I wrote
From the first alphabet.
The first word I spelt.

Raif Kirkul
Instead Of Greeting

Over-dressed in green
The tree was embarrassed,
The stork regretted it all
And returned to his red house,
Winter handed in his resignation
Offering spring his place.

Mevlut Ceylan, born in Ankara, has lived in London since 1979. A poet, translator and teacher, he has three poetry collections in Turkish. With poet Feyyaz Fergar, he founded *Core*, an international poetry magazine, later a publishing house. Ceylan has translated many poets into and out of Turkish, edited two anthologies of Turkish poetry and translated selections from James Joyce's *Chamber Music*, and R D Laing's *Conversations with Children*.

Reputations Recouped

Anne Wilkinson

EVAN JONES

A few years ago, over dinner at his flat in Toronto, I asked the novelist and poet Richard Teleky – in one of those conversations that North Americans do so well, flitting from topic to topic, from the differences between Roman Catholic and Eastern Orthodox funeral rights to visiting Marguerite Yourcenar's home on Mount Desert Island – about the poet Anne Wilkinson (1910-61). Signal Editions of Montreal had just reissued her oeuvre, I remember. 'Oh, she's wonderful,' he told me. 'Someone tries to resurrect her every twenty years or so, but the poems don't take.'

The poems don't take. I've thought hard about this. What it means when being a wonderful poet isn't enough, when good writing doesn't suit an age or a society, perhaps; or a social programme for that matter. Wilkinson was, in her lifetime, appreciated, published, anthologised, but the appreciation, publications and anthologies since her early death from complications due to cancer have slowed and slowed.

In her fifty years, she completed just two books of poems and left a trail of magazine publications. She has been resurrected in book form three times: first by her greatest supporter, the Canadian anthologist and poet A.J.M. Smith, in 1968; second, in 1990, her poems were collected and edited by poet Joan Coldwell; and most recently in *Heresies: the Complete Poems of Anne Wilkinson (1924-1961)*, edited by Canadian Modernism scholar Dean Irvine.

She was not a groundbreaking poet. There are no new, exciting forms here, no real breaks from the past or tradition: Wilkinson is instead tied directly into her age. Stylistically, she was a poet of the then and there. Read her poems and the shade of Dylan Thomas, the most prominent poet of her era, rises and casts itself about. As a young woman, educated and raised in a wealthy, Southern Ontario family (her great-uncle on her mother's side was the physician Sir William Osler, the 'father of modern medicine'), loyal to the flag and the crown (as any good colonialist with a knighted great-uncle would be), Wilkinson would have read Thomas. He toured widely and was *the* poet of the Empire at the time. Another Canadian poet, Daryl Hine, told me how he himself was introduced to Thomas in British Columbia in 1951, when just fifteen. Thomas was not only a poet, he was a presence.

What gets Wilkinson out into the sunshine, however, is the manner in which she shakes Thomas's ghost. Because even as she welcomes the apocalypse, she is frustrated by it, turning and twisting the prophetic with a shake of her head. Hers is what Northrop Frye called a "parody-apocalypse". What I mean by this is exemplified in 'Little Men Slip into Death', a short poem from *The Hangman Ties the Holly* (1955), Wilkinson's second collection. It has to it something of Thomas's 'Do Not Go Gentle', but advances in a very different way:

> Little men slip into death
> As the diver slides into water
> With only a ripple
> To tell where he's hidden.
>
> Big muscles struggle harder in the grave.
> The earth is slow to settle on their bones,
> Erupting into mounds or sprouting flowers
> Or giving birth to stones.
>
> And how to stand a tombstone
> With the ground not quiet yet,
> And what to say, what not to say
> When moss is rooted and the stone is set?

The first stanza has the spirit of Randy Newman's song, 'Short People': there's a meanness in the speaker, who suggests that weaker men just die and leave little trace. The second continues the bias, with its preference for the burly type not going gently into the good earth, it seems. The parody, odd as it is, kicks in the final section, as the poet worries how to stand a tombstone, which even as the ground erupts, sprouts and gives birth, does eventually settle anyways, leaving the stone set. Her whingeing and griping has made little difference: little or big-muscled both leave the poet to consider death and the problem of continuing to live. This is the parody: the mocking of the heroic in Thomas's poem, and most importantly the woman's perspective on such a mode. Though inspired by the poetry of men, Wilkinson was a poet very much concerned with being a woman; she had lived through two world wars and the loss of her father when she was nine. It is clear in all of her poems that a female voice is speaking, and that a feminine perspective on the world itself is called for. She seems almost self-conscious about it, in fact; but is too subtle a poet to be caught out in such a way.

Sometimes, we postcolonial types go looking for writers whose work meets the fashion of the empire. This is as much true of poetry as it is of fashion, music and art; and it's as much true today as it was sixty or seventy years ago (only now we can choose between multiple empires). In a way, in the fifties, Wilkinson was that poet. But in reconsidering her work now, it is clear that she was not some sort of female Canadian disciple of Thomas. We all have our starting points, and living beyond those points is a luxury: just before he died, Thomas confessed to a young Donald Hall that he believed he had not outdone his starting point, Yeats. Did Wilkinson? Her two collections and run of periodical publications are various and vital, full of mythical, metaphorical, and metaphysical work ranging from ballads to riddle-poems to nursery rhymes. Many of her formal considerations are indebted to her reading of Thomas. But that "parody-apocalypse" – and let's be clear: just because she parodies does not mean she aims for humour – separates her work and makes it distinctive.

Her long poem, 'Nature Be Damned', published in a Canadian journal in 1957, but not collected in the poet's lifetime, might be speaking again to Thomas directly, but if so it is a poem of rejection, which Dean Irvine calls 'a curse upon her Green Order':

> And so I damn the font where I was blessed,
> Am unbeliever; was deluded lover; never
> Bird or leaf or branch and bark of tree.
> Each, separate as curds from whey,
> Has signature to prove identity.

'Nature Be Damned' was meant to open her third collection, which was partially assembled in manuscript form when Wilkinson died. It's clear that even as she was acknowledging a debt in this poem, she was also shaking it off. "The force that through the green fuse" drove Thomas is a font for Wilkinson to damn. The title of what might have been her third collection, *Heresies and Other Poems* (there is no poem titled 'Heresies' in the manuscript), tells us as much. But the poem is more complex, because it isn't just a parody of Thomas but of the apocalyptic movement in total. In five sections, the poet moves through the world denying and even destroying nature, but in section five she comes full circle, "Once a year in the smoking bush / A little west of where I sit / I burn my winter caul to green ash". In this final act, which is a ritual itself, "an annual festival", Wilkinson is goddess, reborn and born, mother and child: and so the world itself is reborn. Yet, the final closing couplet draws all this into question – "Then roused from this reality I saw / Nothing, anywhere, but snow" – and she's lost control. Perhaps at this point the poet is not a Thomas disciple at all, but a fellow-traveler, and one who sees and resolves the world very differently. What was parody has become its own poetic. Wilkinson's poems took her beyond the apocalypse, denied it, and ended up in the snow. There's that frustration, that shaking of her head I mentioned. She can't quite believe it herself, and this is what makes her poems unique.

Yet *the poems don't take*. I think I understand what Richard was saying to me. Wilkinson has not been fashionable since she died, true. But she wrote at a time in Canada when our national poetry turned more to Great Britain than the US: a time that the generation before my own turned away from in their search for a more quintessentially Canadian verse. I make this connection now, because Wilkinson did everything else. She had chops and finesse, style, substance and a verse that was steadily and uniquely her own. She fit into her age and responded to it with verve. But sometime after she had departed, her tradition turned just enough in her native country that what she was doing was deemed unattractive. That's a shame, as what falls between the cracks in these kinds of poetical shifts is often worth as much if not more than what comes to the surface.

Evan Jones's second collection, *Paralogues*, is forthcoming with Carcanet.

Between Two Worlds: Poetry and Translation

Between Two Worlds: Poetry and Translation is an Arts Council-funded audio recording project the British Library has undertaken in collaboration with the poet Amarjit Chandan.

The project records for posterity a wide range of poets who have settled in England having migrated from outside the UK and who may be either bilingual or have English as a second language. The project has also recorded some UK-born poets who publish in more than one language or in some way reflect the project's theme of dual cultures.

Each recording consists of a reading of a selection of poems followed by an interview on the personal experiences and situations that may have influenced the poet's creative work.

All the recordings will be preserved at the British Library and may be consulted in the Reading Rooms.

The poetry readings are available to listen to online at: **http://sounds.bl.uk/betweentwoworlds**

An accompanying educational resource for use in schools, and a 6,000 word essay by Amarjit Chandan may also be downloaded from the site.

Moniza Alvi	Moris Farhi	Esmail Khoi
Fadhil Assultani	Saqi Farooqi	Yuri Kolker
Ravil Bukharaev	Omar García-Obregón	Gwyneth Lewis
Oleg Borushko	George Gömöri	David Morley
Amarjit Chandan	Lydia Grigorieva	Mohan Rana
Adam Czerniawski	Choman Hardi	Roberto Rivera-Reyes
Diego de Jesus	Nigar Hasan-Zadeh	Sudeep Sen
Imtiaz Dharker	Liu Hongbin	Saradha Soobrayen,
Eduardo Embry	Kapka Kassabova	Satyendra Srivastava
Kit Fan	Mimi Khalvati	Saadi Yousef

In association with

ARTS COUNCIL ENGLAND

Image of Choman Hardi in the British Library recording studio by Amarjit Chandan.

REVIEWS

I mean instead, seriousness in their drive to be written, a
sense of compulsion and discovery in the process, that
more than carries over into the reading experience.

– Tracy Ryan

This Music Is So Heroic

ALAN BROWNJOHN

Tomas Tranströmer, trans Robin Fulton, *New Collected Poems*, Bloodaxe,
£12, ISBN 9781852244132;
Natalya Gorbanevskaya, trans. Daniel Weissbort, *Selected Poems*, Carcanet,
£12.95, ISBN 9781847770851;
Gjertrud Schnackenberg, *Heavenly Questions*, Bloodaxe,
£8.95, ISBN 9781852249229

Readers in Sweden – but equally many who are well acquainted with his work in translation – have been wondering for some time when Tomas Tranströmer would be seriously considered for the Nobel laureateship. It can only have been an understandable reluctance to make the award on home ground that held the Swedish Academy back, because there has long been a world-wide acknowledgment that no living poet deserved it more. For nearly forty years Tranströmer's poems have inspired translators in other countries – over fifty at the last count – to render in their own languages the compelling images and insights he has derived from coming to grips with the austere Scandinavian landscape.

In these islands, the American poet Robert Bly was the first to publish, in 1972 in a London Magazine Edition, thirty translations of poems chosen from Tranströmer's first five books. In 1983, the same year as the original appeared in Sweden, John F. Deane in Dublin brought out a remarkable version of his ninth short volume, *The Wild Marketplace*. Most recently, in 2006, Robin Robertson translated with striking freshness a small selection from seven books, published with facing Swedish text, by Enitharmon. But from the mid-1980s onwards Robin Fulton has dedicated himself to rendering into English the entire body of Tranströmer's work. The current *New Collected Poems* updates – with a number of additions, mainly short poems written since the poet's major illness in 1991 – Fulton's edition of 1997, which in turn substantially expanded the *Collected Poems* of 1987. It is fitting not only that Tranströmer's achievement should be recognised with the Nobel honour as he turns eighty, but also that the reissue of a volume showing Fulton's incomparable skill and dedication as a translator should so happily coincide with the award.

Robert Bly caught the essence of Tranströmer's poetry in his introduction to the 1972 book, *Night Vision*, where he remembered Mallarmé urging poets to achieve mystery "by removing the links that tie the poem to its occasion in the real world." To Bly it seemed that with Tranströmer "the link to the worldly occasion is stubbornly kept, and yet the poems have a mystery and surprise that never fade." From the start – and Tranströmer retains two items ('Storm' and 'Five Stanzas to Thoreau') from his teens – there is an unmistakeable quality of rigour, spareness and concreteness about the poems. They are a lesson in economy. They resist every temptation to abandon reality and perpetuate the alarming adolescent fantasy (described here in the prose 'Exorcism') in which their author felt "trapped by a searchlight which radiated not light but darkness."

Tranströmer's is a modern rational consciousness confronting the complexities and terrors of the twentieth century world with the help of the particular calm he finds in the seascape of the Stockholm archipelago (which several ancestors worked as seamen; they are commemorated in *Baltics*), its history, its stones and sounds ("You need only close your eyes to hear plainly / the gulls' faint Sunday over the sea's endless parish") – and the quiet of the inland forests. And yet it is the achievement of a poet who has lived in the city, worked in a demanding, down-to-earth profession (as a psychiatric worker with young offenders) and seen much travel and experience elsewhere in Europe, in Africa and in Asia: see 'The [Balkan] Journey's Formulae', 'Downpour over the Interior' (in the Congo) or 'Streets in Shanghai'.

Personal life and relationships make an appearance as sudden overwhelming presences. In 'The Couple', two lovers in a dark hotel room sense that "the town has pulled closer / [...] The houses have approached. / They stand up close in a throng, waiting, / a crowd whose faces have no expressions." And in 'Alone', in the second before a fatal car crash (which in fact doesn't occur), "My name, my girls, my job / broke free and were left silently behind [...] / The seconds grew – there was space in them – / they grew as big as hospital buildings." Is he a political poet? Only if he can be that without slogans and exhortations, just writing compelling, mysterious poems with patent elements of shock and compassion felt on encountering poverty or violence; as with 'In the Nile Delta', or in 'Schubertiana': "'This music is so heroic' [...] / But those whose eyes enviously follow men of action, who secretly despise themselves for not being murderers, don't recognise themselves here, / and the many who buy and sell people and believe that everyone can be bought, / don't recognise themselves here. / Not their music." The "music" of Tranströmer's poetry is in its unindulgent, truthful, moment-to-moment connection with a real world rendered always with what Fulton sees as essential to it: "the very sharply realised visual sense [...] the first-time reader or listener has the immediate feeling of being given something very tangible."

The *Selected Poems* of Natalya Gorbanevskaya in Daniel Weissbort's translations is a welcome updating, with all her books up to 2010 represented. It is a pity that new readers unfamiliar with the the poet's life and work would need to refer to Weissbort's 1972 edition to learn more about her early experiences as a writer and appreciate fully how Gorbanevkaya's dissident activities in the Soviet Union 1968 led to her detention in a psychiatric prison. But the interview here with the critic Valentine Polukhina is informative and revealing, not least for an element of reserve and caution in Gorbanevskaya's responses which also prevails in many of her poems, even after thirty-five years of exile.

All are very short, and nearly all are untitled. Those from the fifties and sixties are coded and muted cries of anguish; a foreign reader needs to listen closely for the implications in her command "Search as you might, hop, don't look round, / like a sparrow on the Hermitage roof. / [...] A battle-tested sparrow like a boat among mountainous waves." There is little optimism or consolation, even of a traditional kind: "Love, what nonsense, / what bird-brained foolishness, / when it's already too late / to spare or pity me." After reaching Paris in 1976 she declares that "to language itself are my due love declarations", but hers – as she makes eloquently clear in a 1983 lecture Weissbort includes here – is the Russian of an exile citing her gratitude to Delaunay, Brodsky and Mandelstam, and with not much to celebrate in her adopted countries. Modestly, Gorbanevskaya concludes that "the linguistic problems of the poet in exile are not so arduous as are the daily problems of life for ordinary émigrés", and it is notable that around half of the poems here are from the last decade. Among them are some of her most clear and candid pieces, and there is even an occasional note of lyrical joy as in 'Three poems about the rain': "those tender, / flowing contacts, that douse heat / and quench thirst... / The cloudmaster has unclenched his fist / and I'll suffer no more."

If elegy in poetry, at any rate in Britain, has in recent decades become more directly personal and intimate in mood and detail – see the way Douglas Dunn, Peter Porter, Ted Hughes and Penelope Shuttle have written about the loss of partners – the American poet Gjertrud Schnackenberg has taken, in *Heavenly Questions*, a step backwards into traditional formality of a dangerously weird and ambitious kind. Four of the six lengthy poems with which she commemorates the dead husband with whom she shared many of these interests address "unanswerable cosmological, philosophical and mythological questions." The two sections most closely concerned with the immediate circumstances of his death, 'Sublimaze' (a painkilling drug) and 'Venus Velvet No.2' (the pencil, or "vein of graphite ore", she uses to note things in the hospital) are much the most moving and appropriate. These at least allow the reader with an ear sensitive to rhythm to forget for a while the monotonously unvarying iambics she has chosen to employ throughout, a medium which somehow sanctions other lapses of judgment: the appearance of "myriads", "infinities", a "wondrous deed" and an "immaterial labyrinth". Schnackenberg's intention seems to be to clothe her tribute in a special solemnity and mystery afforded by these plodding pentameters; a sad mistake, because incantation they might be but poetry they are not.

Alan Brownjohn's latest book is *The Saner Places: Selected Poems* (Enitharmon, 2011).

The Fierce And The Fragile

CHLOE STOPA-HUNT

John Burnside, *Black Cat Bone*, Cape, £10, ISBN 9780224093859;
Lavinia Greenlaw, *The Casual Perfect*, Faber, £9.99, ISBN 9780571260287

English poetry is shot through with a mingled toughness and delicacy, going back at least to Edward Thomas and shaping some of the most impressive new collections appearing today. John Burnside's *Black Cat Bone*, deserving winner of this year's Forward Prize, is certainly one such book. Towards the end of the collection is a poem both ekphrastic and meditative, 'Pieter Brueghel: Winter Landscape with Skaters and Bird Trap, 1565', and as Flemish painting is ruggedly luminous, so are Burnside's eerie, formally exquisite lyrics. This poem articulates an incisive compassion that lies at the heart of the collection, even in poems that inhabit territories of tragedy and sin. Each skater "has his private hurt, her secret dread", an Audenesque isolation of suffering which for Burnside is only the beginning: "we live in peril, die from happenstance, / a casual slip, a fault line in the ice;

/ but surely it's the other thought that matters". *Black Cat Bone* is always open to the poetic possibilities of such "other thoughts" and strange cross-currents. It is perhaps not surprising to find, then, that even in a collection facing up so unflinchingly to loss, the "other thought" here echoes and transforms *The Prelude*'s famous skating scene, offering a radiant and recuperative moment of adult joy that Wordsworth could not have encompassed:

> At midstream, the children play
> with makeshift hockey sticks and, near the church,
> a man finds the thoughtless grace
> of the boy he once was
> to glide free
> in the very eye of heaven [...]

The poems are rich in these meticulously captured moments of being, from the boy of 'Disappointment', "standing up to his waist in a Quink-blue current, // a burr of water streaming through his hands / in silt italics", to the half-lyrical, half-raw simplicity of the union described in 'Moon Going Down'. Here, Burnside moves with a consummately assured touch between a tender rhetoric of loss (his characteristic line-breaks are a perfect formal match for such writing – "that / dove sound caught in her throat / that I thought was ours"), and a more imagistic mode: "they swarm / like bees, // a honeyslick, an / aftergloss of meadow". His formal skill seems to broaden with every book, and he is as adept with the pared, macabre beauty of the short line ("milk on her fingers, / the hurry of pain / in her eyes") as with the emotional ironies of the Pope-like couplets which conclude 'Faith', and which marvellously capture the endless surprises and repetitions of grief.

Black Cat Bone looks searchingly through from birth to death; a shifting, time-freed world where trains, films, and headlamps sit without awkwardness beside witchy talismans, ancient "billhooks and sickles", or the "sheepfolds and clouded byres" of Brueghel's peasant landscapes. Nature is an ardent and dangerous presence in these poems: a realm populated by the lost, where human and inhuman forces meet. At the end of the collection, 'From the Chinese' captures the instant of seasonal change "when nothing to see / gives way to the hare in flight, the enormous // beauty of it", a sight working with irresistible force on the human observer.

The long opening poem, 'The Fair Chase', follows an uncertain hunter tracking an unusual beast. Burnside's reputation as a poet of immanence should not obscure the fact that this poem – and *Black Cat Bone* more generally – takes up its thoughtful residence in the moment of afterwards. The beast itself is there to produce what happens after the beast; the hunter, "alone in a havoc of signs", parses as much as he hunts, an intimate, half-baffled interpreter of everything, from his prey to his own past. 'The Fair Chase' reflects Burnside's earlier work, in which tentative encounters with dead, dying, or elusive animals evoke complex responses, yet the end of the poem opens out into a superlative new vision of the beast's imagined suffering, simplified into pure colour and yearning: "calling for the life it must have had / far in the green of the pines, and the white of the snow".

Lavinia Greenlaw is, like Burnside, an assured practitioner in the music of the unsaid, and her latest collection, *The Casual Perfect*, is keenly aware of the potency of indeterminate experience, particularly memory. "How I fetched up there we do not say", begins 'The Drip Torch', but the unexplained origins of the experience – the speaker helping to complete a "prescribed burn" – are put aside in favour of charting the images of fire-dripping:

> each soft splash igniting
> white as a conjuror's dove
> subsiding into the earth
> making safe the black path.

The opening poem, 'Essex Kiss', sets the tone of Greenlaw's collection, merging a realism shaped from clustered, spiky sense-impressions ("Chewing gum and whelks, a whiff / of diesel, crocus, cuckoo spit") with the speaker's powerful and decisive lyricism: "I will lay you down / on a bed of nettles and blackthorn. / Your body will give way like grain". *The Casual Perfect* seeks out such moments of connection, but apprehends their randomness and brevity. This is the keynote of 'A Theory of Infinite Proximity', which offers a "boundless, bright, defined" image of love's endless imminence: "To always be about to take / a step into the other's arms". 'The Literal Body' is a poem built around psalmic anaphora; mostly in unrhymed two line stanzas, each unit of text begins with "That". At its end, the poem discovers that the connections and unions looked for by speakers in *The Casual Perfect* are sought by others, but that this kinship of longing does not necessarily make them more successful. Therein lies the poem's final note of achingly intimate shock:

> That the displacement of cells
> is a fire in a darkened building

> where against all expectation
> her lover keeps looking for her
> keeps taking her hand.

Greenlaw's poetry is full of doubt and thought; deeply engaged with the process of writing. The concluding line of 'Indigo Bunting' seems to halt and half-correct itself: "I mean I will not speak of this – this colour – again". The line has reached out towards the metaphysical dimensions which underlie this tiny, impeccably pure bird-poem, but Greenlaw changes her mind, tying her words to the specific and descriptive colour of the plumage. In 'Spill', poetry's exactitude (or deliberate occlusion) becomes a game: "The herring is a silver purse, / no longer a purse of silver".

The brief quatrains of poems like 'The End of Marriage' and 'The Catch' are metrically unpredictable, altering their pace to admit half-dissonant notes. In the latter, the speaker tellingly confesses that "It's not the theme that interests me / but the variation". Greenlaw has conclusively mastered the poetry of provisionality, of sidelong looks. Like Burnside's *Black Cat Bone*, *The Casual Perfect* is a beautifully assembled collection, artistic in every sense. Burnside speaks in 'Moon Going Down' of lovers "strung like pearls on molten wire", an image that evokes the vitality and dignity with which these poets string words. Modulating between the fierce and the fragile, time is their canvas – and all of life, fair game.

Chloe Stopa-Hunt is a poet from Hampshire; she won the 2010 English Poem on a Sacred Subject Prize.

Homer And Away

STEVEN MATTHEWS

Alice Oswald, *Memorial*, Faber, £12.99, ISBN 9780571274161

The experience of reading *Memorial*, Alice Oswald's remaking of Homer's *Iliad*, is unsettling, in ways that had perhaps not been predicted by its author. The book continues Oswald's practice of creating "non-dramatic dramas", powerfully conceived in her most famous work, *Dart*, and most recently seen in *A Sleepwalk on the Severn*. But here it takes a radical turn. Oswald's brief, justificatory note explaining her method in the book casts it as communing once more with "the spirit of oral poetry", which she finds to have governed her source text. Yet her way with that 'spirit' strips away the original's narrative drive, and creates instead a 'bipolar' work made up of juxtaposed passages which render biographical laments for the many fallen soldiers from Homer's war alongside developed similes. These similes are freely adapted from Homer's own lines, but are also tuned to the tradition of pastoral lyricism with which Oswald's own writing has consistently associated itself. The opening note to *Memorial* also associates the biographical voices with those of women grieving over the corpses of dead soldiers. Oswald then produces a slightly confusing set of labels for what has been achieved by this method, showing impatience with the notion of "translation" before favouring "translucence", which is glossed as "writing through the Greek".

However, it is difficult to know what is gained, in this case, from this method of shining a light through the primal scene of European literature. Christopher Logue's (in many ways freer) variations on Homer had revealed a violent, imagistic work, with gruff-voiced soldiery and haphazard divine interventions. Anne Carson, recently, has found manifold ways of adapting classical tropes and stories (*The Beauty of the Husband*), but also grammar and syntax (*Nox*), to parallel or counter modern delights and traumas. Oswald's method clearly seeks to rival Carson's approach, as she dares what she calls a "reckless dismissal" of most of Homer's epic in order to isolate the laments and similes. But it's never clear how, in her mind, the associative power of the latter relates to the illuminative potency of gods arriving on earth – which she also claims to wish to reveal in the Homer. If such an arrival is as Oswald, echoing T.S. Eliot and others, claims, an "unbearable reality", it is also the case that her similes are thoroughly composed, rarely oblique or startling – or, that is to say, in this instance, unconventional. Anachronisms are sometimes thrown in gratuitously; of two brothers amongst the slaughtered, for example, we hear that previously they "came home as proud as astronauts". These are hardly as strange or startling as the inclusion of the "patent Frigidaire" by Ezra Pound in his wartime *Homage to Sextus Propertius* (1917).

Against the dynamics of previous versions of the classics, such as those mentioned, Oswald's new book paradoxically advertises its stasis. In place of a table of contents, *Memorial* offers seven pages printed with the names of the dead from Homer's text, each in capital letters, as though on a familiar war monument. Smaller lists naming the killed then punctuate the main text. More awkwardly, and for me unnecessarily, the freely variant similes juxtaposed to the biographies of the dead men are repeated, verbatim, throughout. This repetition of chunks of poetry, sometimes as much as twelve lines long, is presumably intended to add to the gravity and weightiness of the work. But, in the end it achieves the opposite effect. It is hard not to find oneself skipping the repeats as the work goes on. Both these facets, the capitalised lists and the repeated similes, work against "the spirit of oral poetry", and make *Memorial* difficult to voice for contemporary readers. This resistance to accommodation of such loss is Oswald's point, but the necessity to perform it as such length and in such style remains doubtful.

Much depends, then, on those similes, and on what they add to our enduring sense of the horrors of mass slaughter, be it in ancient or in modern wars. Some of these images (ignoring their repetition) are genuinely odd, like the skewed versions of pastoral achieved by Oswald in her earlier *Woods etc.*:

> Like a drop of fig juice squeezed into milk
> Mysteriously thickens it
> As if a drip of lethargy
> Falls into the bucket
> And the woman stirring
> Stops

More often however, in fact almost universally, the similes simply confirm that the perennial violence irrupted within humanity simply mirrors that in a natural world, yet again "red in tooth and claw". In Oswald's version, batterings of wind and waves are perennially "like" those which dint the helmets of the innocent farmers and horse-keepers who find themselves caught in (to them) incomprehensible death. More particularly, those gods she sees as rendering reality "unbearable" are often presented as odd or unpredictable through rhetorical assertion, rather than through full poetic realisation. Lightning, for instance is "terrifying" for a man out walking, who sees the "fields [...] Lit up blue by the strangeness of god".

Memorial, all in all, is a strange enterprise, both in its method and in the results. It does not succeed, for this reader, in helping us rethink our understanding either of war or of Homer, for all the daring of its way with its original text.

Steven Matthews's collection of poems, *Skying*, will appear from Waterloo Press in the new year.

Medium, Conjuror, Flâneur

CAROL RUMENS

Peter Bennet, *The Game of Bear*, Flambard Press, £8, ISBN 9781906601256; Billy Collins, *Horoscopes for the Dead*, Picador, £9.99, ISBN 9780330543736; Ahren Warner, *Confer*, Bloodaxe Books, £8.95, ISBN 9781852249144

Tarot aficionados would have a slight head-start in decoding some of the work in Peter Bennet's opaque new collection, *The Game of Bear*. Mythographies named for the Major Arcana – *The Tower*, *The Chariot*, *Temperance*, *Justice*, etc – are scattered throughout, suggesting a deconstructed sequence. But the Tarot symbolism turns out to be only one layer among many. Despite familiar syntax and metrics, an only-occasionally exotic vocabulary, and roots in the Northumbrian landscape, Bennet's work seems immersed in private or coterie referents.

'The Tower', for example, proves unimpressed by its responsibilities as opening poem. Its texture is tapestry-rich; its assonance as always compelling. The "gasps and hushes / of soot-falls" into hearths "sound like a restless audience" in the opening lines. But "Meanwhile my lady sighs and adds a hiss / and more mist to the mist that lifts / the pele above a curtilage / all evidence for which dissolves in guesses." By now, a certain steaming-up has occurred.

Is the lady the tower, the narrator a chimney-pot ("her walled-up rival")? Is she rain or clouds? And who is the "sweet admirer" watching them? Perhaps it's the Fool from the Tarot Pack. The lightning "fizz" at the end is more recognisable.

Some poems emerge more persuasively into focus. These include 'The Moon', seemingly a delicate personification of moonlight as a ghost-child who skips "in bare feet on the ice to please us" but unlocks more than pleasing imagery when she "skedaddles as she ought / to leave us where we're always left precisely / whenever sentiment resembles art." The Tarot pieces are interleaved with other portraits and meditations: in the first section, there are rather fine studies of Mahler and Unity Mitford, for example. Occasional rhymes underline some almost brutal moments of clarity. 'The Juggler', with its helpful Ewan McColl epigraph "Spring's a girl in the streets at night," finds images of rich and delicate corruption, but the last line wields a battering-ram: "She'll get her kit off when I ask her though." Just as the collection seems composed of one or more deconstructed sequences, many of the poems form deconstructed narratives.

The long centre-piece derives, we're told, from a short story by Sean O'Brien, and a border ballad of dubious provenance. Bobby Bendick is a priest who aspires to forbidden knowledge (Sophia). Dialect quatrains follow him as he gallops hell for leather, like Tam o'Shanter, pursued by a demon. The strophes between these quatrains are brocade-like mystery narratives, in sometimes archaic diction. They are strangely static, layering time into pockets. These arts are not very dark, in truth: a raid on the past to enrich the present moment of contemporary poetry, with some extremely intelligent tourism woven into the narrative. A characteristic rhythmic pattern in many of the book's poems switches between five and four-beat lines. More rhythmic variation might better distribute the expressive load. Bennet's unquestionable verbal talent seems ingrown in this collection, and the complications that fill the poems seem driven less by genuinely difficult ideas than the "fascination of what's difficult."

If Bennet's persona wants to be interesting, Billy Collins's wants to be understood. In fact, he has said in an interview that, when he writes, "I'm speaking to someone I'm trying to get to fall in love with me." His textures are light, and his anecdotes reassuring. Unfortunately, his characteristic narrative swerve from realism to fantasy soon feels formulaic. Another ploy, used in 'Gold' and 'Poetry Workshop Held in a Former Cigar Factory in Key West', is to deny that the poem will contain any poeticisms, while in fact milking the figurative possibilities for all they're worth: "Not once did I imply that tightly rolling an intuition / into a perfectly shaped, handmade thing / might encourage a reader to remove the brightly colored / encircling band and slip it over her finger...". The fantasy episodes vary from the slight and charming to the forced and self-conscious. A small, amusing idea – that shopping for a mattress is hell but not hell as the mediaevals saw it – is not made funnier or more profound by the seeming after-thought of bringing Dante along to lie between the couple testing the mattress. Compare Paul Durcan, ruthlessly effective in this kind of surreal debunkery. Eccentricity can seem merely silly unless raised to the power of vision. 'Grave', in which the speaker lies on the ground to talk to his dead parents, is almost embarrassing. On the other hand, the title poem concludes with a striking turn, transforming the blue-suited corpse into a bird that has flown "straight up from the earth / and pierced the enormous circle of the zodiac." It's regrettable that the thin pathos of the notion of "horoscopes for the dead" has been spun out at such length in the preceding stanzas.

Collins is deliberately working against the pretentious in poetry, but poems may be difficult without pretension, simply because the poet's ideas and necessary verbal ambitions are complex. Having also positioned itself against difficulty, Bloodaxe has made a sensible revision in adding Ahren Warner to its list.

The complexity of Warner's poems often seems the result of a mind pulled between different languages. The languages include other texts: Derrida, Baudelaire, Nietzsche and even the paint catalogues featured in 'Confer', the title-poem. Warner doesn't pursue mystification for its own sake. If he calls a finger-print a dactylogram (he does) it's because the classical etymology better fulfils his analytical and erotic word-undressing: and it makes a link with "pictogramme" and "engram." His persona is a sober flâneur, rarely down but often out in Paris and London. It's that mad muse, language, who makes such an occasion of a late train or a fancied girl. Witty as well as erudite, this muse exploits a nicely low line in high-table innuendo in 'The Carpenters' Arms', where the drunk philosophers take it in turns to pronounce on sex: "Heraclitus implies the clitoris sits close enough to witness / the crux of metaphysics; / a stream in which the fetishist can bathe but once."

Warner is interested in the music of the poem: it may be a 'Sonetto' or otherwise, but it's always a sound. 'La Brisure' finds, after Derrida, the fracture and the hinge in the word, and expresses it in a kind of poetic bell-ringing. Inter-line spaces create rests, as in music, and allow the segments of a sentence to resonate and avoid the desiccation of the line-break. His Baudelairean imitation, 'Harmonie du Soir', with its subtle repetitions and cadences, beautifully opens out the pantoum of the original. 'Troia Nova', a Madoc-ian voyage through literary London, forms the sparkling crown of the collection, its refrain sliding through every possible etymological nuance of the city's name.

In company with many other young poets, then, Warner is influenced by Paul Muldoon. Although the influence is intelligently handled, and suggests a genuine like-mindedness rather than mere imitation, the frequent echoes can seem unrelenting. At his best, though, Warner rows his own coracle, with his own deft motion. It will be essential to follow his voyage through future collections.

Carol Rumens's latest collection is *De Chirico's Threads* (Seren, 2010).

Of Poetic Urgency

LACHLAN MACKINNON

Susan Wicks, *House of Tongues*, Bloodaxe, £8.95, ISBN 9781852249069;
Jane Duran, *Graceline*, Enitharmon, £9.99, ISBN 9781904634997;
Linda Chase, *Not Many Love Poems*, Carcanet, £9.95, ISBN 9781847770868;
Sasha Dugdale, *Red House*, Carcanet Oxford Poets,
£9.95, ISBN 9781906188023;
Kelly Grovier, *The Sleepwalker at Sea*, Carcanet Oxford Poets,
£9.95, ISBN 9781906188009;
David Tait, *Love's Loose Ends*, Smith/Doorstop, £5, ISBN 9781906613358

Susan Wicks's *House of Tongues* covers a wide range of material and kinds of poem. She writes about travel, memory, history, love and death; she moves from elegy and meditative lyric to the sustained sequence.

There are two sequences in this book. The earlier one is about a deer. In the first of six poems, the deer is seen on a day before a storm. During the storm, the poet imagines an "unseen fawn" and feels herself "want to believe / they lie together nestled in a deep / hollow lined with leaves, and sleep out the thunder". There's a fatal sentimentality here, encapsulated in the unsurprising word "nestled". In 'Deer Grazing', the poet runs by her browsing subject. "If I were up close", she imagines:

> I'd see myself red-faced
> in my kit and trainers, pausing to let my heart
> subside in my throat and the day
> tick gently, a plane drifting across.

The self-portrait contrasts with the deer's "soft skin", but neither, except for the heartbeat, is quite vivid. The aircraft hangs as a metaphor, but becomes literal in the next and final stanza:

> That world in her eye
> could crumble, burst into flame,
> and the tiny people float down
> like ash, their final messages
> make rings in her iris as they fly apart.

Are the "they" of the last line the messages or the people – and which, exactly, "fly apart"? The poem blurs. The sheer unlikelihood of a new Lockerbie incident happening in view of this particular deer further undermines the poem's wish to show how nature is better in some ways than human beings. Which is, in turn, not a novel thought. Better, though harder to follow, is the account of human awfulness in the collection's closing sequence, poems drawing on the history of Visby, the Swedish port.

Flat language and fuzzy writing also let down Jane Duran's *Graceline*. Here, she first explores her childhood experience of being taken by her parents from New York to Valparaiso and settling in Chile. But, for instance, describing the sea as "a tremulous, perpetual line" doesn't force us to see more than we know. In 'Like It Is', Duran remembers that "I shared a cabin with my sister", and that by "the coast of Perú, // and near Arica, the stench of guano / reached our ship". The girls could see the "whitened rocks", and as "the sun passed over them / like the flat of a hand" it "drew out a lingering smell". The final line of this poem is "Write about the guano, my sister tells me". She just has: that's all we get. Whether the sister's injunction comes from then or now is an interesting but unexplored ambiguity. Neither are we told why the sister wishes this, or what importance the guano has. The poem doesn't quite add up. 'Invisible Ink', a sequence about the Pinochet years, has better moments; 'Street, Santiago 1973' is gripping in its sketchy evocations of a scene where horror has not yet happened, and the future when "those long hands / at rest in a woman's lap // are wrung". This ending stings.

Both Wicks and Duran are established writers. Each conveys respectable, unstartling sentiments, but without the edge poems need if they are to be memorable – or even, I fear, much re-read. I had looked forward to both their books, whereas I was unprepared for the greater zing of Linda Chase's *Not Many Love Poems*. In a love poem, 'Corsican Summer', Chase remembers that "Once, driving up a mountain in Corsica, / you talked about storms in Colorado / which turned the trees to ice." Wind made "the branches craze / like crystal chandeliers chiming through the night". After a flat, reportorial opening, the poem lifts a little. Placed at the end of a line, "craze" works as an active verb before being made exact. The next line, "You were a kid in your bed, listening" regrounds it. That "your" conveys warmth and familiarity. Now, the poet wants to hear the tale again:

> Longing for cold has swamped me
> like a huge coat, dragged on the ground.
> It's not my coat, my love, and yet
> I want each seam—each buttonhole,
> the buttons themselves. I want that son
> the ice trees sang in the night to a boy.

Here, it's a simile rather than a metaphor that becomes literal. The details of seams and buttons make it actual. As the poem turns into the last line, it seems to lift off effortlessly. Again and again, Chase's poems have a snappy acuteness. In the first stanza of 'Secret', for instance, she sees:

> You, almost fifty, bumming secret cigarettes
> and then shoving mints in your mouth
> as if you wouldn't get caught.

It's funny; the "You" is as much exclamation as vocative. In the second stanza,

> I see the boy in you.
> I want him to kiss the back of my neck,
> then turn around and run like hell.

The poet's imagination carries her with it.

Sasha Dugdale's imagination runs away with her. In *Red House*, the title poem describes a place in which a series of events of different kinds takes place. "Once a man brought home a bear to the red house". As a way of winning a woman's affections, he teaches the bear to dance:

> In an endless manbeast cha-cha, paws clattering, feet slapping
> His humming succour from the stairwell.
> The bear they took on the third day; it went well enough back into the
> light.
> The man threw himself from the window, and he was lamed for life.

This isn't simply surrealism, because it is contained within an authoritative structure. When she takes control back from her inventions, Dugdale is clearer, but I suspect her most serious work is as yet the most impenetrable. Her energy and wit suggest that this is a way-point towards more considerable achievement. I look forward to her next book.

As I do to Kelly Grovier's. He risks the phrase "the slow / emptiness of a poem", but he's better than that. The trouble with *The Sleepwalker at Sea* is not that the poems are empty but that they are too full. Thought is congested, and often I felt that the poems sprang from occasions about which he said too little. 'Lips', for instance, begins:

> This coffee tastes burnt,
> as though it knew something
> about death, the way that stars
> left in the sky begin to know
>
> something about you; and the trees
> have that bitter aftertaste as well,
> what with all that leaving.

This is assured and engaging, if the run from second to third line feels a little plonking. "What is it with the sea", he continues,

> moistening its white lips
> over and over
> like someone getting ready
> to whisper or to sigh?

"Leaving", which means both "bringing forth leaves" and "departure", seems in the second sense to be the emotional centre of the poem. The brightness of the images conceals what is really going on, though. Avoiding autobiography is understandable and often decent, but it can lead to needless obscurity.

Two slightly dull books, then, one that is rewarding, and two that are slightly vexing. David Tait's pamphlet *Love's Loose Ends* contains twenty poems. They appear to be straightforwardly autobiographical, recounting a love-affair. In 'End Credits', he tell us that:

> As for beauty: I think I've experienced
> the moment in life that will flash
> before me at the end. He was on top
> and his eyes were shut, his mouth open
> as if he were swimming: a child again,
> his hair floating around him like seaweed.

Utterly intimate, utterly unembarrassing, this is an extraordinarily poised way to begin a poem. Tait continues:

> Earlier that night we'd watched a movie
> where the newly dead arrived in purgatory
> to direct a short film of their happiest memory.
> It was about coming to terms, and afterwards
> we'd had a fight and made up and had another fight
> as the credits rolled and we tore off our clothes
> and love spooled before us. And we were cameras.

Everything pulls together, not a word is wasted, and the poem convinces me that it needed to be written. Almost the whole pamphlet reaches this standard, with tacit passion and emotional complexity. Tait's dry voice is informed by imaginative pressure and urgency. Out of this batch of books, *Love's Loose Ends* is the one I'll be going back to.

Lachlan Mackinnon's *Small Hours* was shortlisted for the Forward Prize 2010, and he received a Cholmondeley Award in 2011.

Journeys Of Discovery

TRACY RYAN

Angus Peter Campbell, *Aibisidh*, Polygon, £9.99, ISBN 9781846971990;
Luljeta Lleshanaku, *Haywire: New and Selected Poems*, Bloodaxe, £9.95,
ISBN 9781852249137;
Peter Riley, *The Glacial Stairway*, Carcanet, £9.95, ISBN 9781847770790

All three of these collections are strongly grounded in place, alive to the dynamics and operations of language, and reward close, attentive reading. To begin like this, with what they share, is not to minimise their differences – linguistic, regional, personal and stylistic – but simply to note with pleasure the intensity and serious quality of the poetry in each. The seriousness is not necessarily in tone or subject matter, because there's plenty here that's light, ironic, humorous or sensuously enjoyable. I mean instead, seriousness in their drive to be written, a sense of compulsion and discovery in the process, that more than carries over into the reading experience.

Angus Peter Campbell's *Aibisidh* is especially impressive, its power so progressive and cumulative that you feel led to re-read the earlier-placed poems in the light of what's built up by the whole. It's a vivid and highly-textured imaginative world nonetheless conveyed with apparent simplicity – there's a great trust in pared-back language here. I could give any number of examples, but the poem 'O' stands out, its poignancy increased by deft understatement. We know nothing more about the addressee than "you died young", but the rest of the poem rings the changes on the cyclical, the empty, the circular – just the optimal number of resonances for conveying the feel of "the sphere [...] not a mote less broken" for the shortness of that life lost (my gloss is already so much more word-laden than the poem). Similarly, 'Rays' depicts with minimalist precision a moment where the speaker's father is brought to mind by a complete stranger's actions. The artistry is acute. By the same token, habitual understatement can mean that a poem like 'Moving', in condensing such a complex issue as forced clearances, runs the risk of being read as inadvertent apologia for colonial renaming in Canada of already-inhabited places, something surely unintended in a work so sensitive to historic language-loss.

Aibisidh, divided into three parts, contains poems in Scottish Gaelic and English mostly on facing or alternating pages – sometimes translations and I think sometimes equivalents – as well as one poem in Gaelic not translated, and another in Gaelic that's also, pertinently, provided in Italian translation. I can't speak or read Gaelic, but the presence of both languages certainly enriched the reading for me, and invited a kind of bending-back of the attention. For instance, with the book's title poem, which in English is 'ABC', and which is an alphabetically-ordered acrostic made up of song-titles, the reader is (in either language) constrained to contemplate formal factors – the differences between the alphabets, the culturally-specific song titles that must mean each poem is a dynamic equivalent to the other rather than a "translation" – before even contemplating how those titles work to mean by juxtaposition within the poem. And yet in another sense the surface reading is smooth and simple, so that you have more than one layer slipping about at once.

This is only the most striking example of how *Aibisidh* induces multi-directional reading. It's there too at the level of content throughout: a profound sense of temporal connections and even collapse ('I remember / tomorrow. // Tomorrow / I went to school" ['Tomorrow']), whether invoked through changes in technology, memory, the idea of the Resurrection, the clock, or a past, evocative way of naming and managing, as in 'The Old Gaelic Calendar'. I was won over by the energy, intelligence, assurance and at times beauty of this book.

Equally energetic and intelligent, but stemming from another context entirely, is Luljeta Lleshanaku's *Haywire: New and Selected Poems*. These are poems written in Albanian over nearly two decades, and rendered here mostly by Henry Israeli, in tandem with a variety of translators, without any notable loss of coherence. There's a useful introduction to the Albanian background by Peter Constantine, as well as Afterwords by Israeli and Lleshanaku herself.

The centrality of simile in these poems means that they come across into English with one of their major strengths intact. I can't of course comment on what other richnesses (verbal music) may or may not have been altered. Though I've said simile is Lleshanaku's "major strength", and it is often striking and fresh, it's also true that its omnipresence can sometimes grate ever so slightly, as if one is looking for just an occasional variation in approach. But in any case it's never stale, and not gratuitous. At times it's the seemingly commonplace vehicle of comparison that startles – "Betrayed woman [...] like the worn hole on an old belt [...] like a kettle taken off the stove / still steaming" ('Betrayed') – and sets off a chain of associations. At other times the imagery is more complex, and still unexpected – "A felled tree in a forest / hallucinates skeletons / dragged out of the body" ('Chronic Appendicitis')

– and aptly distressing as in 'They Hasten To Die': "shovelling earth on them has become as common / as sprinkling salt on food".

Lleshanaku's poems feel supremely elemental, dominated by trees, birds, sun, moon, night, shadows as well as other effective recurrent symbols – an ill-fitted door, a mother figure, cyclical repetitions like snow and thaw – frequently also drawing on religious motifs. They sometimes trace altered bodily states which are reflected in the external world, and vice versa. Even at just over a hundred and twenty pages of poetry, the collection never flags in interest.

Peter Riley's *The Glacial Stairway* also collects poems written over quite a span, though in this case it's from 2003-2010. It's an engrossing read, comprising long sequences interspersed with well-placed shorter poems, the whole leading us through observations and meditations on various walks and travels both European and American.

The book opens with the title sequence, detailing a walk across the Pyrenees first undertaken at fifteen and repeated forty-eight years later with a diction apparently relaxed yet full of slippage and ambiguities, ironies especially, that make lines and clauses read back against and resonate with each other. Nonetheless, an abiding consciousness of mortality that treads lightly: "Ahead of us, our strength is trailing away". Sometimes lyrical, frequently subtle with internal rhyme, the poem draws a mix of other languages into its mainly English text, as well as echoes of earlier poets and histories. It's dotted with quasi-rhetorical questions, as if the reader might assent or comment; its long lines are spacious, roomy, meditative, and we feel present in its making.

If there's any one feature that could describe the whole book apart from the idea of journey, it would be this focus on process, on making, which is generously shared with the reader both in unpretentious commentary and by the inclusion of various stages of an idea's development. Many examples could be given, but the most striking is in the book's last pieces, 'Western States (1)' and 'Western States (2)'. Both come from a journal of travel across parts of the United States. The first is written in block or paragraph form, each number referring to a page of the original notebook. These often read as powerful prose poems in themselves, and the effect is cumulative. The second is a set of mostly two-line, well-honed poems – more primal, sparse and oblique now – drawn from the paragraphs (though not always mapping exactly onto them): a work related to the first and yet entirely different. (I happened to read them in order; it would be interesting to do the opposite, too.)

In general this work's self-awareness means it has already ironised and has factored-in the difficulties of writing about "other" places. A good deal of informed scrutiny feeds the commentary of 'Western States (1)', though I wonder if any degree of summary or irony can adequately broach the over-determined problems raised by, say, part 50, which concerns a particular group of indigenous Americans seeking to have "the USA's biggest spent rods dump sited on their land, for the sake of the rental". The issue doesn't benefit from condensation, and scare quotes around the chosen word "miserable" are not quite enough. But on the whole, this is work that doesn't shy from the difficult aspects of relations to place. Like Campbell's and Lleshanaku's, it offers a wealth of insights into poetic technique as well as subject matter.

Tracy Ryan is a novelist and poet from wheatbelt Western Australia. Her most recent book is *The Argument* (2011).

Expansion And Intercession

W.N. HERBERT

Thomas Lynch, *The Sin-Eater: A Breviary*, with photographs by Michael Lynch, Paraclete Press, $22.99, ISBN 9781557258724;
Tony Williams, *All The Rooms of Uncle's Head*, Nine Arches Press, £6, ISBN 9780956551474

These two slim collections are both bursting with ideas and possibilities. Each focuses on a distinctive outsider – in Lynch's collection *Argyle*, the eponymous sin-eater, in Williams's the unnamed inhabitant of an unidentified asylum – and frames their portraits or monologues with accompanying materials which enhance the reader's experience.

Lynch, famously also a Michigan undertaker of Irish descent, juxtaposes his accounts of Argyle's travels and travails with images by his sons: mostly photographs by Michael Lynch. These have a curious effect on the poems: on the one hand 'setting' them in the distinctive landscape of the West Clare Peninsula, where the Lynch family came from; on the other creating a narrative reliance on the image to illustrate or amplify each particular text, which is not always met.

Meanwhile, Williams constructs an ingenious and elaborate imitation of Outsider Art: his protagonist has made a series of ceramic tiles on which the poems – essentially a sonnet sequence about his incarceration and psychosis

– are framed by a running commentary, on several levels, which requires the reader to rotate the page to keep up. The text is literally unsettled by the act of reading. To add to this physical deranging, the 'tiles' have apparently been 'smashed' at some point, and their reconstruction is not always complete: cracks run across the pages and jagged sections are blacked out here and there, leaving us to guess at occasional phrases.

These are complementary but contrasting ways to augment the act of reading a poem, and carry the risk of overwhelming the text – if the proper centre of our attention is accepted as being that text. If it is not, then these collections should be understood as repositioning the reader's experience as something balanced between text and image, or between text and concept.

In Thomas Lynch's case, the presence of an 'Introit' discussing both the poet's relationship to Catholicism and to County Clare, and the concept of the sin-eater, makes it clear that there is a metaphoric relationship between the Irish-American undertaker-poet and the scapegoat figure he introduces via The History of American Funeral Directing and its magnificent "Puckle tells of a curious functionary, a sort of male scapegoat called the 'sin-eater'." Lynch emphasizes his character's outsider status by giving him a definitively Scottish name: "after the socks, of course, the only thing I knew that was reliably Scots, apart from whiskey, and the acoustic resemblance to 'our guile'". Of course, "whiskey" is exactly not "reliably Scots"; Scotch is, in Scotland, spelled "whisky", but these tiny shibboleths are part of the estrangement Argyle experiences. He is precisely a secular paraclete, forgiving those the priesthood cannot bring themselves to forgive:

> [...] Argyle refused their shilling coin
> and helped them build a box and dig a grave.
> 'Your boy's no profligate or prodigal,'
> he said, 'only a wounded pilgrim like us all.
> What say his leaping was a leap of faith,
> into his father's beckoning embrace?'

This of a suicide. In another passage, he lambasts the clergy as "red cassocked dandies and mitered wankers, / the croziered posers in their bishoprics" before letting rip with a graphic comparison neither narrowly: "For all their vesture, rings and unctions, / preaching to bishops, like farting at skunks, was / nothing but a mug's game to the sin-eater." In skunkless Clare, this little Lowellesque incomer can only have a metaphoric existence, one more readily available to an American audience than to an Irish or British one.

There is, then, a type of cultural gap over and beyond the space Argyle occupies between the sacred and the sacerdotal; this being the gap in the poet's own identity between Irish and American. The book's photographs usually bridge but sometimes emphasise this gap, as in the picture of Thoor Ballylee which accompanies the poem just discussed. For many, the Yeats tower plus the castigation of bishops equals Crazy Jane and those magnificent, disturbing lines, "Love has pitched his mansion in / The place of excrement". But, although Argyle reflects in a similar mode elsewhere, here image and text and allusion feel separate rather than synergistic, as though we're simply being shown an image from the environs of the verse. Elsewhere, however, glimpses of low stone houses and elemental landscape, memorials and votive shrines, serve to position the fugitive insights of the troubled shamanic figure of Argyle, perpetually on the move between villages and between worlds:

> Outstretched on the strand, his body's immersion
> in the tide was not unlike a christening:
> two goats for godparents, two herring gulls
> perched in the current his blessed parents,
> a fat black cormorant the parish priest [...]

Williams' speaker seems to have taken too much to heart Michael Donaghy's remark in *Wallflowers*, "consider how any printed page of verse or prose, with all its paraphernalia of paragraphs, running heads, marginalia, pagination, footnotes, titles, line breaks and stanzas, can be understood as a diagram of a mental process." His poems are accompanied by just such a paraphernalia of devices, each with their own internal laws, which have to be granted (almost) equal status to the poem itself. There is a border text, running around the four sides of the page, often containing a quoted passage along the bottom and left margins. The title is given in a very large font split equally above and below the poem, and the stanzas of the poem itself (often an inverted sonnet running 3;3;4;4) are gathered in braces (those curly brackets), with descriptors or comments written at ninety degree angles to accompany each. The effect is of a text exploding beyond the limits of the poem but just being contained by the further frame of the tile/page.

Each element therefore plays a role in this mysterious speaker's narrative. He is locked in a battle, of and for his wits, with the recurrent figure of the 'Professor' ("Professor Bloodless nodding, poking through / My things"), reflecting angrily on his 'Uncle', who may be responsible for his incarceration ("A straggle of ivy / Turns grey in the dusk. He is smoking merrily"), and dreaming of the lovely inhabitant of cell 36:

> The gravestones are covered in violet flowers –
> Her pubis is covered in violet flowers –
> The pastures are covered in violet flowers –
> I would prefer not to talk about her ankles.

This is a hugely complex apparatus to bring to bear on a relatively short sequence of poems, and it is a considerable achievement on Williams's part that it never overwhelms the human matter at the heart of his sequence. Indeed, the effect is rather like that of reading the nineteenth century artist Richard Dadd's poem which attempts to explain his painting, 'The Fairy Feller's Master-Stroke', painted while in Broadmoor for murdering his father. You feel compassion for the person trapped at the heart of his own unresolvable convolutions of thought.

Of course a great deal of careful artistry has gone into creating this illusion – we catch the little echo of Rilke's first Duino Elegy in one of the framing fragments, 'IF I SCREAMED', and the use of insect imagery to embody the nadir of his psychosis cannot help but recall Kafka:

> BLACK-FIGURED. Chitinous of thought,
> Love-fearing. So I am. And from each wound
> I bear, exude a hæmolymphous spit,
> Simple and inhuman [...]

The difference between Williams and Lynch is more a matter of contrasting goals than one of methods. Each seeks to augment the poem with the presence of other elements, but Michael Lynch's photographs confine themselves to being, beautifully, illustrative. Williams' marginalia, on the other hand, appear to have a more radical goal. Not made in a different medium from the poem they frame, they seem to deepen our understanding of how a poem works, bringing to the surface those phrases that, we suspect, always haunt the phrases that we read on any page.

That it takes the device of a madman's smashed tiles to make these darker subtexts visible points to something you feel both poets would accede to. It remains the poem's task to intercede between that which can and that which cannot be said.

W.N. Herbert's latest collection is *Bad Shaman Blues*, shortlisted for the T.S. Eliot Prize.

Thirteen Ways Of Writing The Non-Poem

TODD SWIFT

Chus Pato, *Hordes of Writing*, trans. Erin Moure, Shearsman, £8.95,
ISBN 9781848611672;
Matthew Caley, *Professor Glass*, Donut Press, £10, ISBN 9780956644503;
Siddhartha Bose, *Kalagora*, Penned In The Margins, £8.99,
ISBN 9780956546746;
Paul Bentley, *Largo*, Smith/Doorstop, £5, ISBN 9781906613372;
Wayne Holloway-Smith, *Beloved, In Case You've Been Wondering*, Donut Press,
£5, ISBN 9780956644534;
Luke Wright, *The Vile Ascent of Lucien Gore And What The People Did*,
Nasty Little Press, £5, ISBN 9780956376763;

Most readers of British poetry would now agree, I think, that there is a spectrum of poetics from, shall we say, Wendy Cope to J.H. Prynne – with Paul Muldoon somewhere in the middle – and that each of these ways of writing poetry has its advocates and its critics. While a recent review of a Charles Bernstein collection in *PN Review* could dispense with this master of American Language poetry by deriding the work as failing to be poetry at all, in general, tolerance is a bit more finely tuned than that, these days.

After all, have we not been co-opted into this idea of the "hybrid" poem – a beast that, unlike the Hydra with its many heads, seems to be a creature with less than one, a sort of compacted melange of various twins and opposites, mashed into a grossly simplified state of settling for the median? Oren Izenberg, in his new study of the divisions between radical and traditional poetries (Princeton, 2011), *Being Numerous*, makes the astonishing claim that the way to resolve such cleavages is to posit a poetry that transcends the poem (non-poem) or in his words: "*what the poet intends by means of poetry is not always the poem*" (italics his). I am not sure about this. Few if any poets set out to write a hybrid poem, or a non-poem, or a poem that lazily fence-sits. Poets find their certain pleasures or their purposes in particular radical, or more traditional, zones of comfort or discomfort. What it seems to come down to, in the end, is how one feels about the lyric form, and how disruptive one should be about (or with) it. Despite Izenberg's idealistic urge to move beyond style, poems have a texture and a taste grounded for most readers and writers in how language does something to the world, and vice versa, not how a poem, like Superman, zooms beyond the stratosphere where diction, syntax, sound and sense, do their stuff.

Chus Pato's *Hordes of Writing*, translated by Erin Moure, Quebec's preeminent lesbian-feminist avant-garde bilingual poet (a hybrid identity if ever there was one!), occupies the most extreme zone of disruption of the collections under consideration here. Much experimental poetry feels as egoistic in its claims as Rap: as if the genre demanded the most radical poetics do-able, with attendant dismissal of the enemy – the canon, the Lyric. Pato's writing is composed, mainly, of sentence-like lines that together formulate a position paper on what poetry, and the poet is, thus, should be:

> Instead of letting the world into the poem
> the poet kicks writing out, like a soft and transparent lava, a muslin

or:

> theory is that ethical violence of the intangible

or:

> 1st Proposition: the true poet is the one whose muse has been
> integrally destroyed

A leading Galician poet, Pato is oddly engaged by romantic notions of the true poet, the muse, and the intangible, for someone who is apparently "kicking writing out" – and to where, and to what end? She writes that "language is as dense as resin" in the long sequence 'We Wish We Were Birds and We Don't Like Binoculars' but also that "paper doesn't last" – so that the tension between a medium (language) of weight, and its dissemination into the world (ink on fickle paper) creates a melancholy, or perhaps, an exuberance, based on this ephemeral position.

Perhaps Izenberg's idea, borrowed from Bloom, of the non-poem does make sense in the light of such writing. Moure's claims for Pato – "Pato wriggles out of any known form of the poem" or "topples all lyric convention" – are pure World Wrestling Federation to me. This book does no such thing. One "known form of the poem" is the open one and, at least since Olson and more recently Carson, little can surprise us on the page through typography alone. *Hordes of Writing* often went over my head but I did find it well-paced, amusing, and, when not simply sententious, rather lyrical, as in "Flowerings of thought, of waters, of sky / absorb." Clearly organised around a deeply-read intelligence, and driven by an *écriture feminine*, this is a destructively integrated muse.

Matthew Caley, a good poet who seems to me to have been under-valued, has, in his fourth collection, gone full tilt at the Theory windmill, as his Quixotic hero *Professor Glass* comes up against the giants of contemporary post-structuralism, their texts, and residual implications. This is a very British take on the post-modern, the deconstructive, with one foot in the camp of the satirist, the other acutely aware of all the signs and signifiers; so it feels a bit like Auden doing Marx, or Freud, except one isn't sure if Caley is of the devil's party or not. The poems are quite formally adept, and, in the manner of Muldoon, their default setting privileges sinuous syntax and intricate rhyme patterns, as if the human mind could be mapped by a virtuousic poem: the sort that, lately, Don Paterson has come to make his own. 'The Lilo of Contingency', perhaps the best in the collection, features stanzas like this (which ends that poem):

> That time is already, er, upon us,
> and as to rapidly summarise
> is the same as to, er,
> erase,
> I am resigned to inhabit the half shallows
> er, where all this starts
> adrift on the lilo of contingency

I am not sure that spoof internal memos, and poems about Walter Pater, and 'Undressing Kristeva', are not more Kingsley Amis than *Glas*, but this is a dazzling book of LitCrit poems.

Siddhartha Bose, a poet who grew up in India, is one of the better of the "Voice Recognition" Poets identified in what seems like a never-ending series of Bloodaxe and Salt anthologies identifying this new British generation of "twenty-first century" poets: a generation perhaps best typified as exponential. Bose is also a "hybrid" poet, in the post-colonial sense of the term. His work in *Kalagora* aims to merge, bridge, fuse, and intertwine (as they say), the diction, themes, and experiences, of various centres, some cosmopolitan, others less so, in a far more earnestly engaged (and academic) way than Daljit Nagra does. It may be a rule of thumb that the more experimental the poet – the more serious – the less funny.

This is the kind of poetry with yin and yang in it. And lots of indents. I find its aims admirable, and its execution adept. The collection's strongest poem, with its rich tangle of language and registers, is likely 'Animal City':

> Twin-bride of my ten-head home, I
>> watch you closely from the
>>> cross of scorched lands, rubble of sea-foam,
>>>> fire of snake-tongue.

> Grand and pungent in act, I long to write you an epic
>> worthy of our ancient tales.

Paul Bentley's *Largo* may not be key to locating the best way of modulating the British avant-garde voice, though this smart, rollicking pamphlet ends with a poem expressly dedicated to Muldoon, the stylistic benchmark for so many, 'Barnsley Abu (a postcard to Paul Muldoon)'. Bentley has his own style, or at any rate, has not approximated Muldoon's quite yet:

> Latest lesson in abjection, perhaps even have felt a slight pull
> on your heartstrings
> as the last of their fans disappear after those two pale
> [...]

But the off-rhyme of pull/pale shows this to be a more formally conservative sort of *jouissance* than Pato's, for example, would ever want to be.

Wayne Holloway-Smith's *Beloved, In Case You've Been Wondering*, is a bijoux pamphlet of crafty, cocky poems that explore a sort of late-Victorian dandyism by way of Babyshambles. This is performance poetry that has learned to charm the page, as is much of the new young British poetry; as if Billy Collins and Carol Ann Duffy had merged into a new poetic whole. Luke Wright, too, is a performance poet, but this time one in the BBC Big League. His pamphlet from (no joke) Nasty Little Press features a bio note to end all such notes with the claim that Wright is "poet-in-residence on Radio 4's Saturday Live, regularly broadcasting to over two million people". Two million people who never buy poetry pamphlets, it has to be said, alas. Still, that's an audience to conjure with. His long poem, 'The Vile Ascent of Lucien

Gore And What The People Did' is artfully stage-managed cod-Byron by way of Auden, written in "ottava rima" and aimed at Politicians with a capital P. It should certainly be put in a time capsule, so much is it of the moment:

> They hacked at local budgets and they shattered
> the public arts. They throttled Northern towns.
> They said disabled children were a matter
> for their parents. Raised premiums on gowns
> and mortarboards. Supped champers as they battered
> the SureStart scheme and shut job centres down.
> Let multinationals feast on comprehensives
> slashed corporate tax at rates that were offensive.

It isn't quite *Hugh Selwyn Mauberley*, is it? Nonetheless, such on-the-nose writing hits all the targets, a quasi-poetical tour-de-force of blunt force rima. So, then, are there thirteen ways of writing these non-poems?

Todd Swift is a Lecturer in Creative Writing at Kingston University; his most recent collection is *England Is Mine* (Punchy Books, 2011). He is co-editor of *Modern Canadian Poets: An Anthology* (Carcanet, 2010).

Adventures In Language

DAVID MORLEY

Daljit Nagra, *Tippoo Sultan's Incredible White-Man-Eating Tiger Toy-Machine!!!*, Faber, £12.99, ISBN 9780571264902;
Rita Ann Higgins, *Ireland is Changing Mother*, Bloodaxe, £8.95, ISBN 9781852249052;
Jean 'Binta' Breeze, *Third World Girl: Selected Poems*, with DVD, Bloodaxe, £12, ISBN 9781852249106

Ben Wilkinson observed how Daljit Nagra's first book *Look We Have Coming to Dover!* (2007) explored the complexities and difficulties that occur in the meetings of differing cultures and languages. In this new collection, such 'meetings' have grown into highly developed harmonies between what Nagra calls Punglish (Punjabi English) and several varieties of

English, phrases of which are invented for the occasion: "the podge of your cheek", "skonked on the hearth", "where dawn Himalayas through Poobong", "the Waltzer armchair of a tunk-tunk-tunkety / train that ptooooums off its tracks" (I counted those o's and u's). Such playful construction is even there in the book's title, with its arrow-shower of exclamation marks.

Tippoo Sultan's Incredible White-Man-Eating Tiger Toy-Machine!!! is a finely-wrought collection that is, at times, tremendous in its daring and sense for the possibilities of form. Nagra's poems perform like spillages of mercury: quick-silver events that brilliantly hold their shape while remaining unstoppably in motion. He unleashes dialects and idiolects that chase around each other and collide (often with a *boom!*). Yet these collisions coalesce, gaining force in poems such as 'The Balcony Song of Raju & Jaswinder', 'Our Daughter, the Bible Flasher!' and the brilliant sequence 'Father Figures' ("You loved it when he came home legless / from The Six Bells / in his dentedly driven Mustang"). Nagra is as ultra-inventive with the sounds of English as he is with his macaronic Punglish. It is as if he is discovering a language within a language. This makes for a surprising and artful experience, but also for something far more unexpected, far more affecting than any special effects.

For example, 'Raju t'Wonder Dog!' is written in the idiolect of Avtar, a Huddersfield shopkeeper. The poem is addressed to his wife, Sapna ("She'll be seen / as havin' dodgy karma by t'community / fer 'er past-life sins made 'er barren") and his faithful Alsatian, Raju ("mebbe he's secretly / t'incarnation of some 'indu God"). The mercurial dialects of Punglish and West Yorkshire slip and crash across the board of a simple and affecting love story with much unsaid and understated:

> From time ter time she'll say: Get thee sen
> a fresh bride who'll production line
> fer you an heir! Who'll get our 'ard earned
> dosh, eh? Raju?
>   By t'way 'soofna' means 'dream' –
> a bit like Sapna in't it? That's why Raju
> and me'll stoop and I'll say: *Sapna,*
> *you're me soofna. Why would I do*
> *owt like to upset me soofna?* Chucklin'
> she'll add: *Aah Avtar, you're me avatar.*
> T'customers'll coo or look reet confused.

Linguistic fireworks, sure, yet I cannot but be touched by how Sapna offers the Alsatian their inheritance even as she speaks her heart to her husband; and how the faithful mutt then mimics the master in consolation. The speaker presents a fleeting picture of tenderness, inches short of sentimentality. Nagra understands that this is the place where most people live and feel and he is not afraid to risk a visit. This is where Nagra has really stepped up. *Tippoo Sultan's Incredible White-Man-Eating Tiger Toy-Machine!!!* realises epiphanies of understanding from a super-controlled collision between voices and cultures. It is a linguistic CERN laboratory of a book, and highly to be recommended.

Rita Ann Higgins has been publishing impressively and always to advantage for more than twenty years. Her subject matter is Ireland and the Irish, and she writes with frankness and force in a free verse that takes on the modulations of declarative speech. *Ireland is Changing Mother* is the first book of poems I have read that takes inspiration from the crash of the Celtic Tiger economy. When the wind of outrage gets behind her pen, her poems on the subject possess energy, vision and attack:

> it was swine flu
> it was birdie flu
> it was real male
> it was single male
> it was jingle mail
> it was Biffo's budget
> it was Robo cop direct / not
> it was bailout or pale-out
> it was paper profit
> it was cranks, it was foreign-owned banks   ('The Darkness')

I imagine some of this material could catch light during a spoken word performance (so long as it was not to an audience of rogue traders). These polemical poems are less craft-driven than the lyrics concerning place, despair and regret. Rita Ann Higgins does not mash-up her languages to create the sonic-boom effects of Daljit Nagra. Her strategy is to place Gaelic in such a context that it surprises and illuminates, almost as if a single word were a poem in and of itself, placed and found in the public setting of a poem in English:

Go to Tuar Beag and sing for her.

Take only left turns
pass out the whitethorn
but remember to pay homage,
admire it as it should be admired
pay no heed to the piseog brigade.

Stay with her *lon dubh*, perch and be ready.
Watch out for straws in the wind
eggs shells, a lone magpie
a wendy goat, mistletoe out of season.

(*piseog*: superstition; *lon dubh*: blackbird)   ('Edict')

The Jamaican dub poet Jean 'Binta' Breeze has been called a "one-woman festival". This most unusual and vibrant writer has never taken an obvious path with subject matter. She might explore her spirituality and sense for sisterhood – but also her own suffering through schizophrenia. She's as wonderfully unpredictable as she is utterly convincing, and this *Selected Poems* is timely and well-chosen. Her poetry shares some of the macaronic urge that we see in poets like Nagra and Higgins, but music and message remain at the heart of her enterprise. Jean 'Binta' Breeze is one of our finest communicators in the spoken word as an art form, her dub techniques both craft and vehicle. One might argue that the current renaissance we are enjoying in spoken word performance would not have happened had she and Linton Kwesi Johnson not broken the ground for us all: even so-called 'page poets' who are now committing their work to memory. Updating Chaucer's Wife of Bath, she writes:

My life is my own bible
wen it come to all de woes
in married life
fah since I reach twelve,
Tanks to Eternal Gawd,
is five husband I have
                    (if dat is passible)
          ('The Wife of Bath speaks in Brixton Market')

Third World Girl is a glory. The DVD includes two readings given by the poet at the Y Theatre in Leicester, and an onstage interview with Jane

Dowson: a beguiling package of material that will persuade you that 'Binta' Breeze is a major poet, and certainly as experimental a maker of word and sound as any L=A=N=G=U=A=G=E poet.

In some ways, all poetry is patois. At best, poetry seeks to push far beyond standard language, or at least to bend it or turn it on itself. All three books under review deploy non-standard English overtly but effortlessly. They are as welcoming as they are challenging to readers. Yet once you move beyond the extraordinary effects of language, what is most alive and memorable in these books is the creation of story.

David Morley's new collection from Carcanet is *Enchantment*. He is Professor of Writing at the University of Warwick.

Five Debutants

LEAH FRITZ

Ian Pindar, *Emporium*, Carcanet, £9.95, ISBN 9781847770653;
Kate Potts, *Pure Hustle*, Bloodaxe, £8.95, ISBN 9781852249038;
Ellie Evans, *The Ivy Hides the Fig-Ripe Duchess*, Seren, ISBN 9781854115461;
Will Eaves, *Sound Houses*, Carcanet, £7.99, ISBN 9781847771124;
Nerys Williams, *Sound Archive*, Seren, ISBN 9781854115386

First collections sometimes include poems that go far back in a poet's writing life. A few in Ian Pindar's *Emporium* may have been written when he was at university: in 'Monsters of Philosophy' the poet tears into some fictional professors. The final stanza suggests that Ian Pindar, like the Elizabethan Sir Francis Bacon, may have gone to Trinity College, Cambridge:

> And still the ghost of Francis Bacon
> Haunts the winding stair below
> Doomed for a certain term to stuff
> A chicken carcass full of snow.

That Bacon died of pneumonia contracted while assessing the insulating properties of snow. *This* Pindar is an erudite poet: a designation once applied to the late John Heath-Stubbs, who strongly objected to it, believing that his sources of knowledge were available to all. Be that as it may, Pindar does provide notes for his 'Chain Letter', a one hundred and eleven line virtual PhD thesis in which each line is cribbed from a different poet, progressing chronologically from William Langland (1332-1386) to Maxine Chernoff (1952-), Heath-Stubbs not included. When you get past this academic glitter, there is real gold in this volume. Although many of Pindar's poems are informal, it includes a fine satirical sestina, 'Les Vacances de Monsieur P.', an off-beat sonnet sequence, 'The Prophecies' and an impressive pantoum, 'Death of a Senator'. His interests are broad, his responses to them musically gratifying and emotionally and intellectually deep.

Pindar's inspiration comes from the fragility of life, his atheistic conviction that death is just that. I was bothered by an underlying sexism in several poems, but in 'It Takes a Man', recognising the origins of this prejudice, he makes an effort to overcome it. Whether or not you share his views on God, the Monarchy or women, I expect you will be moved by the eloquence in much of Emporium. I was about to say that Ian Pindar is a promising poet; but, no, he is already a significant one.

Pure Hustle, by Kate Potts, includes a poem called 'The Runt,' about a small, crippled Greek god. A narrative poem in couplets, it draws on her imaginative insight and apt, surprising images to dramatise his case – "His own, stranger talent befell Him / slowly, with the odd geometry of waking in an unfamiliar room" – and ends comfortingly: "He found, / noticing the dropping sun one harvest night, he had / no memory of that other life, the story of his boyhood – only white noise, / the odd grand smash of godly thunderbolts. No faces and no names." Potts delights in describing what are often small, everyday things, giving them haloes, as in 'Camera-snapped Psalm'. 'A Partridge – A Pear Tree' ironically de-haloes a tired Christmas carol:

> His is a glistering, brass whirr
> of wings, a glide – a chestnut tail.
> I put by the feathers;
> ease the meat from the bone.

In calling her first collection Pure Hustle, Potts has perhaps defined her poetry: the rush of words, ideas, associations; the intense work that must be involved; and even an occasional con trick (the lyrical line which cuts off a political argument at the end of 'November 5th', for instance). In 'Against Poetry', her answer to lines from Percy Bysshe Shelley's 'In Defence of Poetry', she seems to doubt herself: "I am never Persephone, always blustering, and bones." Not true. Her writing is graceful, elegant and witty, albeit maybe not Shelley... yet.

After two books with intricate lacings of self-conscious craft, *The Ivy Hides the Fig-Ripe Duchess* is refreshing in its surface simplicity. The title poem has nothing to do with a duchess, fig-ripe or otherwise, and Ellie Evans quotes from *Hamlet* at the end (always a bad idea to quote a poet with whom invidious comparisons are invited) and she has gone in for 'surrealism' (as Ian Pindar put it, 'Everybody's Talking About Antonin Artaud'): but you shouldn't judge a book by its title – or by what's said on the back cover. Evans's associations are always logical, even in this poem about the end of the world as she imagines it. "After the first purges, the fields were full of corpses / whose nails went on growing, curling into the earth like sickles", it begins, and moves on to leftover typewriters, etc. Nothing spectacular, but well made.

I especially like 'Ant in Vaseline', with its metaphorical insect on a microscope slide, and its conclusion:

> That's how I hurl myself, my jaw agape,
> against my see-through ceiling,
> see-through jelly walls,
> my see-through floor.

There's an amusing sonnet, 'IKEA Room Set' and a deliciously sweet 'New Curate at Llanina':

> Acknowledged suitor now, he comes at twilight
> picking his way between the corn stooks
> because he's carrying a tray of rings
> which wink and sparkle as the darkness grows.

A fine two-part sequence about time takes its title, 'The Bald Sexton,' from Shakespeare; but never mind. Ellie Evans's poetry sings without pretension.

Appropriately, I read 'Salomon's Offertory' in Will Eaves's *Sound Houses* during some noisy refurbishment of the flat above me. "For what infernal place and organ of distempered uproar could be more sweet," he writes, "but what we have not yet in our sound houses? And this quiet fury of discovery call we Pandemonium." During the builders' lunch hour, I picked up the book again to read the charming dream-poem 'Skimpole Abroad,' Here Harold (vide *Bleak House*) has been transported to a mental hospital in Russia:

> [...] His need's
> The gloating of a sun-plumped innocent.
> And all his tenderness the sweet self-praise
> Of one who calculated, giving to be given.
> Harold flounders, protests his love for me,
> For you. For the *borscht* in our veins.

In some of Eaves's lines I hear the ghost of Eliot. Is it the rhythm or the content? I'm not sure. This is from 'A Year Later,' the last poem in *Sound Houses*:

> And when a likeness raises you
> (My rookie laugh, the waft of tea
> Carried outside) we're not surprised
> Though I have learned to be discreet

Will Eaves is at his best when his rhymes, if they exist, are less than obvious. I particularly like his 'Spider', for its acute observation of detail. There are subtleties in *Sound Houses* that should reward many readings.

Nerys Williams tells it differently. Most of her poems in *Sound Archive* are made up of brief unrelated aphorisms and observations, which she streams together to make some kind of sense, perhaps; certainly their confluence makes music. In 'The Dancing House', dedicated to Josef Capek:

> He tells me of sound wave terrorists at sea
> breaking the whale's song
> distressing the dolphins
> changing their acapella to frenzy

Which is combined, later in the poem, with "there will always be spring / there will always be a curator" and, still further on, "Beware of telling the tide to sing / since whoever lies is not believed / even when speaking the truth." Altogether, it is quite a lovely evocation of the house of the Czech artist and writer, and Williams's reaction to it. She also writes, "I am not a sociable person – I do not think so. / I am not a brave person – I do not think so." This "I" may not be Williams – but in her acknowledgements, thanking *Poetry Ireland* for a prize, she writes "The recognition encouraged a shy poet." It's hard to tell whether time spent in Berkeley, California influenced the feyness in her writing or she has been blessed by the Welsh or Irish fairies, but a certain other-worldliness combines well with a vigorous realism to tease the reader into putting two and more than that together to perceive something rare and beautiful. Read 'Shopkeeper's Ledger'; 'The Pedagogical Poet'. ...By all means, encourage her.

Leah Fritz's *Whatever Sends the Music into Time: New and Selected Poems* will be published by Salmon in Spring 2012.

Many Mansions

SARAH WARDLE

Leontia Flynn, *Profit and Loss*, Cape, £10, ISBN 9780224093439;
D.M. Black, *Claiming Kindred*, Arc, £8.99, ISBN 9781906570460;
Justin Quinn, *Close Quarters*, Gallery, £10.50, ISBN 9781852355081;
Ailbhe Darcy, *Imaginary Menagerie*, Bloodaxe, £8.95, ISBN 9781852249014;
John Montague, *Speech Lessons*, Gallery, £10.95, ISBN 9781852355166

*P*rofit and Loss is Leontia Flynn's fine third collection and contains poems of hope and despair, as if reckoning life's balance sheet. An outstanding, Audenesque long poem, 'Letter to Friends' makes this book essential reading, as it brilliantly captures the Zeitgeist. It moves from a personal clearout of belongings hoarded over the last two decades to a review of social and technological advances, financial and political shifts, then moves back to the personal, the loss of her father to Alzheimer's – "My father's wits have flown away like birds" – and the gain of her infant daughter: "my baby daughter too now lies at ease; [...] our lives stand waiting, primed for compromise".

Elsewhere the book includes a poem on the peace lily for Michael Longley, versions of Catullus, musings on living spaces and touching poems on family, memory and motherhood. Flynn has a light touch when describing ill fate, such as that of her schizophrenic uncle, "unlucky thirteenth" child and a forceps delivery administered "too tightly". In 'Reminders' are the lists of bin collections, times of Mass and prescription drugs, with which the poet's parents "measure out their hours [...] regular as tides". However, her assured voice also chronicles such joys as how a plane makes its way, while her baby daughter looks up, "into the beginning of memory".

Claiming Kindred is D.M. Black's first book of poems since his *Collected Poems 1964-87*. He writes with a generous heart, wisdom and at times humour. This volume's opening poem is a moving tribute to both his scientist father and the beauty and wonders of nature which can be rationally explained, yet also experienced with apparently redundant emotion. While he knows about chlorophyll, pollinators and so forth, he sings of how nature causes "the heart to respond with an ecstasy that does not beget children". He also writes of his father's four-year absence on duty in the Second World War, the strain this put on his mother, and of the couple's lives, compromised for the sake of their children, on the father's return. Black records with humour a visit to an attractive young woman doctor, love and sex in older couples – and the poem that he has been rewriting all his life, a plea for his mother's attention. A witty, satirical sequence sees Birmingham as much a character as a place. The poet reflects on humanity on the eve of the Iraq War, but his philosophy is an optimistic one: "I know I cannot fall / Out of connectedness". It is this sense of connectedness that gives his writing affirmation, depth and truth.

Close Quarters is the formalist Justin Quinn's fifth collection. He gets up close and personal with his native Ireland and adopted Prague, describes the Cold War and all the quarters of the year, and embraces the tensions of married life and parenthood. In 'The City Gates' he describes how almost twenty years ago he set about building a life abroad: "I knew / a girl, some words in Czech". Marriage is depicted in a handful of poems, of which it is 'Living Room' that haunts, with parents' arguments making their children imagine monsters and werewolves downstairs, though these have been killed by morning. His is a singing line. In 'Seminar' he "carries America into these young heads" before they trek "across a continent and ocean home". Poems of youth and place are at once private and direct. He recalls details such as the pane of glass in his childhood home's front door that turned everyone to "corrugated shadows" and remembers the pop concerts, at which "we saw the country start to have some fun". Deft lyrics conjoin serious content with mood music, perhaps none more so than the closing poem, 'Elegy', where "parents, lovers, sisters, brothers / are nothing but the print / they've left on others" and children, initially curious about the dead, soon go back to the cartoon, or games of tag.

Imaginary Menagerie is the debut collection of young poet, Ailbhe Darcy, who grew up in Dublin, has travelled widely and now lives in the States. The book is bursting with inventive phrases and viewpoints, as if each poem were a wild animal from the menagerie of her mind. She has abandoned Celtic cadence and metaphor for semantic leaps and juxtapositions and belongs not only with the Irish poets, but in the internet school: a poet who grew up with a global as well as national experience and who speaks the vocabulary of technology, texting, social websites and web design. These are poems of youthful exuberance and travel to give your mind a workout.

In contrast, *Speech Lessons* is the latest volume from celebrated octogenarian John Montague. He writes with uncanny accuracy and affection of family, landscape and traditions, from a boyhood dip in the Liffey to playing King of the Castle atop piles of peat turf with its "cathedral smell". The collection's title poem for Michael Longley depicts a coming of age in Ulster, when he is encouraged to read poetry aloud. An elegy for a resigned President of Ireland alludes to other public speaking. Montague remembers both his paternal grandfather, a JP, and grandmother, who had several children before dying in childbirth, bringing to life their characters in priceless memories of a bygone world.

The poet was brought up in his grandfather's "house of many mansions" by two aunts, one of whom, he recalls, discarded a bunch of wild flowers he had brought her, because, "no longer / a dancing girl / given bouquets / by gallant men", hers was a larger hurt. He has a dig at Thomas Hardy for writing love poetry only after his wife's death, compares this with W.B. Yeats' brimming love poems, and blames Hardy for influencing Philip Larkin's negativity. Montague himself, by contrast, writes with optimism, warmth and skill as he reflects on private and public histories. The 'Speech Lessons' of his title are voiced in each poem: the speeches he puts into the mouths of his cast of family and friends; and the lessons and wisdom he hands down.

Sarah Wardle's most recent collection is *A Knowable World* (Bloodaxe).

ENDPAPERS

Acquire long and lustrous false nails.

– *Ruth O'Callaghan*

The Big Stage

RUTH O'CALLAGHAN

This is Poetry's Coming of Age and *you* – delete Duffy, move over Motion – have been chosen to offer the Word unto the world. A world far removed from that traditional English poetry venue, the back-street church where two old men and a snoring dog have taken refuge from the rain. This is another world, one we all dream foolish dreams about. *The Big Stage.* Hundreds of adoring fans – well, one presumes that they're adoring – packed tight as proverbial sardines and prepared to hang onto every pearl of wisdom that drops from your lips.

But, forgetting aforesaid lips are as dry as a camel in the Sahara, have you really considered the actual logistics of performing in a huge space?

First: clothing. Check the exact length of the astronomically expensive skirt you have purchased to enable you to float gracefully onto the stage. Do not let it become entangled in those matching stilettos you have also bought, as this will give "tripping lightly onstage" a whole new meaning. Indeed, prior to taking to the boards, examine them. That one-foot wrenching movement as you attempt to discreetly dislodge your heel is less than elegant.

Your slim volume has been the subject of long angst. It still is. But the wait until the publisher actually redeemed his promise and published was as nothing to the wait in the wings before facing an audience large enough to fill a West End theatre. Acquire long and lustrous false nails. Coat them with arsenic. This will ensure resistance to nibbling or – in the event of a disastrous reading – a certain end to your troubles.

Your entrance will be no quick shuffle across the floor of some dubious pub, nor the traditional stumble up the steps at the Torriano. No! Traversing The Big Stage from the wings to the mike may not take quite as long as declaiming an entire sonnet – say, whilst swigging the last of the Christmas sherry or doing the ironing – but emotionally it's the equivalent of dragging a fully-laden sledge across the Antarctic.

When you reach your destination you discover the volume of which you're so proud is so slim that it positively rattles in your hand, and that the noise of each shaking page is amplified by the oh-so-sensitive microphone. This is where your pre-performance inter-personal skills will be rewarded. Your success, or otherwise, may well not depend upon the polished perfection of your verse. It is more than advisable to have made friends with the sound engineer, who may well be (let's say) at least one sixteenth Irish (or

Mongolian, or Japanese, or East European). Nurture those roots! Entwine them vigorously with your own even if your name is Smith and you've never set foot on (for example) the Emerald Isle. Said engineer will be fully cognisant with your (lack of) microphone experience from the first strangulated words that you attempt to pitch to the back of the auditorium. But mutual heritage ensures that his skills will be fully utilised for your benefit, and that any residual resentment from the Battle of the Boyne will be buried, as you are not responsible for the carelessness of parents who conceived you on foreign soil.

The sound engineer will probably be in some sort of relationship with the dressing room attendant. Thus, whilst silently noting the absence of a star symbol on the door, the paucity of flowers and lack of a fruit basket, on no account comment. Merely indicate an appreciation of her understanding that this simple, nay Spartan, environment allows the creative impulses a free rein which would not be possible if it were cluttered with extraneous trappings. You may request water. If you are offered wine or champagne, refuse: she has probably earmarked the complimentary bottle for a post-show celebration with the sound engineer. Simply say your vocal chords require the purity of spring water. Do not specify which spring.

Above all, do not allow the pre-show interview to faze you. Inevitably you will be asked if you have previously experienced such huge audiences. Pause, consider for some moments and then name some obscure location with a reflective "Mmm. That *was* big...".

Ruth O'Callaghan has three collections and was awarded a gold medal for her poetry in Taiwan. She has recently completed a successful tour in the States.

JOIN THE
POETRY SOCIETY

Membership of the Poetry Society
helps poets and poetry thrive

*"If you love poetry, we'd love to have you as a member.
With our key publications, **Poetry Review** and **Poetry News**, events,
competitions, exciting promotions and expert advice, we'll put you
at the heart of what's happening in contemporary poetry."*
– Judith Palmer, Director

Poetry Society annual membership includes four issues
of *Poetry Review* and *Poetry News*, discounts, special offers,
poetry competitions, poetry groups near you, monthly
E-Bulletins – and much, much more.

Membership (inc. Poetry Review)
UK from £40 • Europe from £50 • Rest of the world from £55
Concessions available

THE
POETRY
SOCIETY
www.poetrysociety.org.uk

Contact Paul McGrane, Membership Manager
+44 (0)20 7420 9881 • membership@poetrysociety.org.uk